Rommel
The End of a Legend

Rommel
The End of a Legend

Ralf Georg Reuth

Translated by

Debra S. Marmor
and Herbert A. Danner

HAUS
BOOKS
London

Originally published as
Rommel. Das Ende einer Legende by Ralf Georg Reuth
© 2004 Piper Verlag GmbH, München

This English translation first published in Great Britain in 2005
and reprinted in 2009 & 2010 by

HAUS PUBLISHING
70 Cadogan Place, London SW1X 9AH
www.hauspublishing.com

English Translation
© Debra S. Marmor and Herbert A. Danner, 2005

The moral right of the authors has been asserted
A CIP catalogue record for this book
is available from the British Library

ISBN 978 1 905791 95 8

Printed and bound by J. F. Print, Sparkford
Cover image: ullstein bild

Contents

Introduction

Erwin Rommel is undoubtedly the German military commander of the Second World War best known in the United Kingdom, as most books about the Field Marshal were written by English historians. All these works focused on the North African campaign of 1941/42. These battles were of particular importance to Great Britain for two reasons. First, the defence of Egypt and the Suez Canal, and the whole British position in the Mediterranean with Malta and Gibraltar forming the western flank of the Empire, was strategically vital to the outcome of the Second World War. Secondly, after Dunkirk, North Africa was the only land theatre of war where the British confronted the Germans directly. Both these reasons explain the special British interest in the war in the deserts of Libya and Egypt, and thus the scale of Rommel's fame.

Rommel – The End of a Legend is not just another biography in the traditional sense. In this book the most important and at the same time hotly-debated questions on the topic of Rommel are treated in five chapters which build on each other to form a complete picture. In contrast to a full-length chronological biography, such a presentation enables us to clarify connections for the reader and thus draw a more sharply-defined portrait of Erwin Rommel, the man who became world famous as the commander of the Afrika Korps, both as a soldier and as a man.

In the following pages, answers are given to questions regarding Rommel's relationship to National Socialism, the relative value of his North African operations to Hitler's overall strategy, his importance to wartime propaganda, and also his participation in the military resistance to Hitler. A book about Rommel would naturally be incomplete if it did not deal with the development of the myths and legends that surround him. His former British opponents played a central role in this. Even during the war Churchill paid Rommel the highest respect. British commanders like Auchinleck acknowledged him as an exceptionally capable and chivalrous soldier, after the demise of the Third Reich. Not the least reason for this was the desire to portray their own victory in North Africa in an even more positive light. This British respect, in the end, contributed to the post-war reconciliation with the former enemy.

It was Rommel's enemy in North Africa who restored some measure of unsullied military honour to the Germans, in the persona of the Field Marshal – a kind of rehabilitation that was accepted gratefully in view of the war of extermination in the East. The result of this was an idealisation of Rommel, which was increased following the rearming of West Germany and its entry into NATO. Rommel and the chivalrous battle between 'Desert Foxes' and 'Desert Rats' formed a kind of link in the new military partnership between the British and Germans. The fact that it was also Goebbel's propaganda that elevated Rommel to greatness did not fit this picture and was consequently suppressed. Instead, the Field Marshal was transformed into a belated resistance fighter against Hitler.

Rommel's tragic death, by poison sent to him by the Dictator in October 1944, supported this fiction.

But the point of this book, despite what its subtitle might suggest, is not to topple a military monument from its pedestal. Nor is its intent to point a moralising finger at an exceptional soldier, which Rommel undoubtedly was. That would be as disingenuous as the now common tendency to view history, particularly when it concerns the Third Reich, exclusively from the perspective of its end, thus presenting that result as the only conceivable outcome of its beginning. This perspective may support prejudices or world views, but will never do justice to historical figures.

In this book, the intent is to report soberly how it was, always guided by an awareness that historical events can only be understood in the context of their times. Rommel, too, was a child of his era, the product of his generation and constrained by the thinking and behavioural patterns of the military leadership of his time. The pressures tied up in this, which are barely conceivable from today's perspective, contributed to turning decision-making into a true personal test. And there is another factor which should not be overlooked in order to reach a fair judgement on Rommel: his own inadequacies and his contradictions; as well as his dreams and illusions, his ability to be deceived and to deceive himself.

Ralf Georg Reuth
Berlin, Autumn 2005

1

Hitler's General

ommel and Hitler first met in the late summer of 1934. Rommel was in Goslar, where he commanded a Jäger battalion. The 'Führer' had come to attend a Reichsbauerntag (a traditional fair for farmers and landowners that had been transformed into a political event). Side by side, the two men inspected the guard of honour in front of the Kaiserpfalz, the old Imperial palace. They were brought together by the ceremony, but they were very different in their upbringing. The one was an army officer with a strict conception of service, duty and honour. The other was his commander-in-chief, an obsessive gambler, whose ostensibly revisionist politics hid the lunacy of a racially-motivated programme to conquer the world. The two might have seemed, and indeed believed, that they were quite different, but in fact their lives had many connections. On that day, they could not have guessed how fate was to bring them together.

The First World War Veterans

The battalion commander and the Reich Chancellor belonged to the same generation. They were born, in 1891 and 1889 respectively, in a Europe possessed by ultra-nationalist sentiment.

Everywhere people passionately committed themselves to their national identity, searched for their common roots, and tried to define themselves as a national community. The best example of this was the Austro-Hungarian Empire, where a variety of cultures had been forced to live under one government. This feeling of national folk identity was probably why Hitler, as early as his Vienna days, had dreamed of uniting all Germans into one nation, uniting German-Austria with the German Reich. Otto von Bismarck, the 'Iron Chancellor', had already started the process by forming the German Reich from the previous patchwork quilt of states including Württemburg, Rommel's home.

In addition to nationalism, the period when Hitler and Rommel were growing up also exhibited a strong desire for imperialism. The old Habsburg monarchy was experiencing internal difficulties due to its multi-cultural nature, and was content to confine itself to maintaining its continental super-power status. But Germany, on the other hand, lost no time exercising its imperial ambitions. Once the army had paved the way to the establishment of the Reich, and Kaiser Wilhelm II had succeeded to the throne, Germany commenced building a powerful navy to secure its 'place in the sun', alongside France and Great Britain.

Most Germans viewed participating in the pursuit of this imperialistic goal as a patriotic duty. Any belated doubts seem to have been submerged by a strongly-felt sense of 'Germanic' superiority. Hidden by this common dream of a German world empire, opposed by the existing world powers, a conflict was brewing between the upper class, which had their status enshrined by the anachronistic three-class voting rights of the Reich, and the working, underprivileged masses.

His final report from the Officer Cadet School in Danzig said 'fit for military service': Rommel as a cadet, 1911.

The nation staggered into war in 1914 as if it were drugged. None of the European nations, including Germany, wanted a war. However, as each nation's mobilisation triggered the mobilisation of the next, war became inevitable. Germans forgot their internal differences and perceived the war as a release, an opportunity to burst their confining chains and escape the choking second-class position their country found itself in. The German Reich would quickly win the war and rise to unprecedented greatness. Memories of the Franco-Prussian War, coloured by romantic illusions of heroism and invincible prowess in battle, obscured the reality of the modern world. No one could have foretold the incredible destruction and mass slaughter the industrialised world would produce.

9

And so a whole generation of innocent young men, hungry for adventure and praised by their homeland, marched off to a war beyond anyone's imagination, one that would change them decisively. Amongst those men was young Lieutenant Erwin Rommel, a platoon commander in Infantry Regiment 124 König Wilhelm I, based in Weingarten, a garrison town in Swabia. Rommel described the mood in the barracks on 1 August 1914 before his regiment entrained: 'All the young faces shine with joy, enthusiasm and thirst for action. Is there anything more beautiful than to face the enemy at the head of such soldiers.' On the following evening the regiment marched out of town for transport to Ravensburg with 'resounding music and straight step. The population of the town escorted them in their thousands. An unending stream of military trains were already rolling at short intervals towards the threatened western border. Amongst ceaseless hurrahs, the Regiment departed as night approached.'[1]

Among them was the former inhabitant of a shelter for the homeless, Adolf Hitler, to whom the war offered a most welcome opportunity to leave behind the failure his life had been so far. Despite his Austrian nationality he had succeeded in enlisting as a volunteer in the 16th Bavarian Infantry Regiment. He was transferred with this regiment to the Western Front in the second half of October 1914. The 'most unforgettable and greatest time of my earthly existence' had now begun, Hitler declared, and he was convinced that in contrast to this 'colossal struggle' all that existed before would fade into 'shallow nothingness'.[2]

The eyewitness accounts by both Rommel and Hitler show the idealism and naïve expectations with which young men like them went to war. Rommel reported that he feared arriving too late for the first battle. Likewise Hitler wrote in *Mein Kampf* of his expectant train ride with enthusiastic Bavarian infantrymen along the Rhine and then towards the west: 'A single worry tormented me during that time – me, as so many others – would we reach the Front too late? Time and time again, this alone kept me from finding any rest.'[3]

The gruesome reality of war that confronted the ignorant idealism of the troops, symbolised by the sacrifice of the German student regiments at Langemarck, served to weld millions of fighting soldiers together in a common destiny. Their violent experiences of war and the ever-present spectre of death – whether marching in the direction of the Meuse in the autumn of 1914 with Rommel's Weingarten regiment or in the 'steel hurricane' of the first battle of Ypres that Hitler experienced – served to remove barriers of class and transport them to what seemed another world. Only this communal spirit gave each man the individual strength needed to stare death in the face, as, for example, during the assault in Flanders' fields where, as Hitler later described it, 'an iron greeting came whizzing at us over our heads'.[4]

Both men not only survived but also proved themselves year after year. Not only that, they also demonstrated extraordinary and unexpected courage. The draft commission in Salzburg had determined in February 1914 that Hitler was unfit for both 'combat and support duty'.[5] And Heaven knows the military career of Erwin Eugen Rommel, the son of a grammar school teacher from Heidenhiem in Swabia, did not start with great promise. The 18-year-old grammar-school student applied for entry in the Imperial Army only with reluctance, on the insistence of his father. He applied to the Artillery, Engineers and Infantry; the Artillery and Engineers rejected him, but the Infantry accepted him, and in mid-June 1910 he joined his regiment in Weingarten. In March of the following year he was posted to the Königliche Kriegsschule in Danzig where he completed the nine-month officer training course. The training officer who gave him his final rating believed Rommel to be an 'average' soldier. He was 'fit for service' and 'of sufficient intellectual disposition', as was noted succinctly on his graduation certificate. But he had already caught the attention of his instructors at the cadet school with his eagerness, his 'strict sense of duty' and was repeatedly evaluated as having 'great strength of mind'.[6]

That strength of mind would mark Rommel during the First World War as an outstanding troop officer. He was outstanding as a platoon leader in the bitter battles of the Argonne, where the Württemburg regiments under General Mudra gained a special reputation. Rommel described the bitter battle, as well his unshakeable determination 'never' to retreat from the enemy, in his after-battle reports written in the 1930s and published as a book under the title *Infantry Attacks*. He described an encounter that took place near Varennes at the end of September 1914 as follows: 'A small group of my former recruits presses through the undergrowth with me. The enemy is firing rapidly again. There, finally, I see five Frenchmen in front of me, barely twenty paces away. They're standing up, shooting offhand. My rifle is at my cheek in no time. Two Frenchmen, standing one behind the other, fall as my shot cracks through the air. I shoot again. The weapon jams. I rip open the bolt quickly. It's empty. There's no time to reload in the face of the nearby opponents. There's no cover nearby. Withdrawal is out of the question. The only option I see is the bayonet . . . The enemy shoots as I attack.

12

Hit by a round, I now tumble and lie a few paces from the enemy's feet. A bullet, entering from the side, has shattered my left thigh. Blood spurts from a fist-sized wound. I expect another shot to finish me off at any moment. For minutes I lie there between the lines. Finally my men break through the brush with renewed hurrahs. The enemy retreats.'

In October 1915 Rommel, now a company commander, joined the newly-formed Württemburg Mountain Battalion, which had received its baptism of fire in the High Vosges against French alpine infantry. It had proved itself so effective that it was to be used subsequently whenever an elite attack unit was needed in mountain warfare. In the summer of 1917 Rommel and his men fought the Romanians in the mountain range of Cosna (part of the Carpathian Forest), and eventually in October of that same year found themselves at the Isonzo Front. The Italians had been slowly but surely pushing the Austrians back, fighting eleven bloody battles since their entry into the war in May 1915. A newly-formed German army was now supposed to push the Italians back over the border towards the River Tagliamento in the Twelfth Battle of the Isonzo.

It was during this battle that Rommel's 'heroic attitude to life' (as it was described later) made him a war hero. In January 1915, he had been the first of the lieutenants of his regiment to receive the Iron Cross First Class. This time the Kaiser was to decorate him with the Pour-le-Mérite, Imperial Germany's highest decoration. After a breakthrough battle at Tolmin in October 1917 Rommel and his mountain troops scored an impressive victory. His unit, functioning as the spearhead of the German Alpine Corps, had captured the towering 1,600-metre high massif of Monte Matajur southwest of Caporetto two days after the beginning of the offensive. This had taken a

The 'Pour-le-Mérite'.
Rommel was decorated
with Imperial Germany's
highest military medal
in 1917.

massive effort of willpower. Rommel's men, in an uninterrupted battle, 'carrying heavy machine guns on their shoulders,
[overcame] an altitude difference of 2,400 meters climbing
and 800 meters descending and covered a stretch of 18 kilometres as the crow flies through uniquely hostile mountain
defences.'[8] His battlegroup, composed of only four companies,
overwhelmed five Italian regiments in surprise attacks before
finally attaining the strategically-important peak. 'At 11:40am
on 26 October 1917,' Rommel wrote in his book, 'three green
and one white flare signalled that the Matajur Massif had fallen.'[9]

Shortly thereafter he commanded an assault detachment that
took the strategically-important village of Longarone in the
Piave region, cutting off the Italians' retreat. His men took over
8,000 prisoners as a result of this attack, and he once again
showed that he was a bold, determined and clever commander.

Rommel showed a 'shining courage' wrote one of his fellow officers. 'Despite the greatest strains, he possessed apparently inexhaustible strength and freshness, an ability to put himself in his opponent's mind and anticipate his reactions. His planning was often surprising, intuitive, spontaneous and not immediately transparent . . . Danger did not seem to exist for him.'[10]

From January 1918 Rommel watched the outcome of the final decisive battles of the Western Front as a First Lieutenant on the staff in Germany. This same Western Front was where Corporal Hitler found himself campaigning. He fought with extraordinary daring at Montdidie-Nayons at the end of the last German offensive between Soissons and Reims, an offensive which had brought them to within 60 kilometres of Paris. A Jewish officer recommended him for the Iron Cross First Class. He was given the decoration, rare for an enlisted man, in August, and was cited in Regimental Despatches as having been able to get important messages from Regimental Headquarters through to the troops in particularly difficult circumstances.

By this time Corporal Hitler had experienced four years of the problems and privations of an infantryman in war. He had fought in 1916 in the Battle of the Somme, in 1917 in the Spring Offensive near Arras, and in the autumn of the same year at the doggedly embattled Chemin des Dames south of Ypres. Like Rommel as a junior officer, this 'quiet, somewhat unmilitary-looking' man, for whom the uniform was the 'holiest and most cherished',[11] had summoned up an unbounded determination to manage his existence as a runner, whose life expectancy was so short. And like Rommel, the presence of imminent death had given him a sense of fatalism, the same sense that shaped the emotional irrationalism of so many of his generation. The courage and callousness with which they both moved under the heaviest fire gave them an aura of invincibility among their comrades. Rommel's men considered him bullet-proof, attributing this to his instinctive ability, his sixth sense, to anticipate what his opponent would do. On the other hand Corporal Hitler's comrades believed, 'When Hitler is along, nothing can happen to us.'[12]

Rommel and Hitler had each individually drawn the conclusion that they must be under the protection of the Almighty. They had been wounded several times, and had escaped death by a hair's breadth dozens of times. This provided Hitler with the driving force for his later sense of mission, while for Rommel this manifested itself in his actions as a troop commander, where he was sometimes irrationally optimistic in his evaluation of tactical options. Both of them had the self-delusion that, in the end, one's own will is always the determining factor. Consequently, their experiences at the front made them what they were. In brief: the war was their life; and the army was their home. 'Without the army, none of us would be there,' Hitler once wrote.

The Consequences

The sudden end of the war with the defeat of Imperial Germany and the Revolution in November 1918 was a major shock for soldiers like Hitler and Rommel. After four years of fighting their 'glorious army', in which they had served and which had become their home, fell apart. Nothing seemed to remain of the great classless patriotic solidarity which they had experienced in the trenches. Instead these men realised it had all been for nothing. The decorations for valour they had so proudly worn were worth no more than the tin they were punched out of. 'And so it had all been in vain. In vain all the sacrifices and privations; in vain the hunger and thirst of months which were often endless; in vain the hours in which, with mortal fear clutching at our hearts, we nevertheless did our duty; and in vain the deaths of the two million who fell,' Hitler wrote in *Mein Kampf*. His words described the feelings of a whole generation.[13]

Something dreadful, something inconceivable must have happened. After all the German armies were still deep inside enemy territory when the all-powerful military leadership abdicated and handed responsibility over to the politicians. It was devastating to see Matthias Erzberger, the representative of the new Reich government, go to the forest of Compiègne to sign a humiliating armistice, one that resembled capitulation. They could not admit that the superiority of the enemy had become overwhelming after America's entry into the war. Nor were they aware that the home front's resources were almost exhausted and that civilian deprivation there was spurring the almost-forgotten class conflict, a conflict brought into sharper focus by the Russian Revolution.

The possibility of civil war haunted those men who had held their posts at the front and now were returning home to an estranged and apparently dissolving world. They were confronted by a yawning void. They felt deceived, and looked for someone to blame. It could not be the army in which they had served; they could not allow that. So they found it in the red revolutionaries, and by extension all democratic movements. These were the forces that wanted to remove the monarchist order, and more importantly for them, reduce the important role of the army. Blinded by their feeling of betrayal they refused to acknowledge that the Social Democrats were in fact engaged in a bitter conflict with those who wished to convert Germany to a socialist republic on Soviet lines. Many returning soldiers and millions of nationalistically-minded Germans on the home front believed with indiscriminating prejudice that the two were indistinguishable, and that their common betrayal of Germany had led to the disaster. Early on the 'Stab in the Back', which never happened, would form one of Hitler's 'final truths', and after it had gained general credence in right-wing thinking, even reached the apolitical Rommel.

For both men, as for their entire generation, the after-effect of this supposed betrayal, as well as the real social disorder, was traumatic. The Republic, which had been declared by the Social Democrat Scheidemann, seemed to be infected by a deadly divisive virus. It seemed to those who had experienced the solidarity of trench warfare that everyone in this Republic was fighting each other. The civil war lunatics of the post-war period seemed to provide proof of this infection for both Rommel and Hitler, particularly since they both confronted them first hand. Rommel led his company in a bloodless confrontation with red councils in Lindau in 1919. Later he was posted to the Ruhr where a red army was responsible for fomenting unrest. While a member of the Munich garrison Hitler participated in the suppression of the First and Second Bavarian Soviet Republics by the Reichswehr and the Freikorps. The need for national unity thus became a decisive legacy of the World War not only for these two but also for so many others – a legacy Rommel was to give voice to beseechingly again in 1944 when he told a comrade that it had to be ensured that in any future defeat the nation would not fall apart again.

In the year of the revolution of 1919 Hitler's career in politics began, which for him was no less than a continuation of the World War. That year saw the victorious powers imposing new borders and excessive reparations on the vanquished through the Treaty of Versailles, the Russian Revolution spreading the octopus-like tentacles of Bolshevism from the east toward Central Europe, and a feeling of doom spreading through the starving German populace. Under the influence of nationalist sectarian circles, which attempted to blame 'International Jewry' as the puppeteers behind Bolshevism and Revolution as well as the Versailles Diktat, he would commit himself to the struggle against this 'global enemy' with the same determination he had demonstrated at the Front. The goal of this struggle was to save Germany, even Europe, and eventually the whole world from the 'World Jewish Conspiracy', which he believed was responsible for pushing Germany into disaster. The ideology of his racial obsession would eventually become the motivating force in a political programme conceived in the mid-1920s and set out in the two volumes of *Mein Kampf* and a further, unpublished work.

Drawing on his experiences during and after the war, Hitler wrote of his conception of a tightly-knit national consciousness, in which there would be no more artificial social barriers and snobbery and in which every German would be able to identify with the Fatherland. The foundation of this vision was the recognition that the old order of Imperial Germany had proven itself to be outmoded. The aristocratic ruling classes had clung to their established positions with as much arrogance as ignorance, ultimately showing their inadequacies by their failures in the war. 'I would make their leaders responsible for these soldiers killed in action,' Hitler had occasionally said to amazed comrades in the trenches.[14]

19

Hitler wanted to replace the old order with a modern society similar to the well-oiled clockwork of a machine. Forced into line and of racially pure, Nordic stock – this society would be a match in the fight for survival and the racial struggle against the 'Jewish World Enemy'. This 'modern society', in which there would be no room for the weak, the 'unworthy', and above all Jews, would have to follow a rigorous programme to be able to win a position in the forefront of the 'eternal struggle of nations'. He also firmly believed that the laws of evolution gave the strong the 'right' to expand at the expense of the weak. Hitler's intention of expanding to the east towards Russia resulted from his thinking on the errors of Imperial Germany. However, he considered the Kaiser's policy of building up a strong navy a even greater error. That policy had the effect of ensuring Great Britain's hostility, whereas Hitler would have wished to have her as an ally.

Rommel is unlikely to have heard anything of the Austrian ex-corporal's theories in the 1920s. Neither the bourgeoisie nor the Reichswehr took Hitler seriously, viewing him as just another nationalistic anti-Semitic sectarian. Consequently his *Mein Kampf*, which Rommel is unlikely to have ever read, went largely unnoticed. However, Rommel too had taken to heart the humiliation of the nation as a result of defeat. He was particularly unhappy about the 'ignominy for the Fatherland' perceived in the 'Diktat of Versailles', especially the 'War Guilt' clause which denied the previously glorious army its moral integrity and reduced it to a skeleton strength of only 100,000 men.

The exaggeration of the issue, the conspiracy theory, which seemed unique to Hitler's mania, was not in Rommel's nature. He was not one of those hopeless and blinded have-nots who believed that the 'Man with the Moustache' would bring them

He showed her the battlefields of the Isonzo and Piave after the First World War. Rommel and his wife, Lucie, circa 1918.

salvation and redemption. After all, Rommel had remained in the army and was therefore removed from the struggle for survival. In October 1920, six months after Hitler was demobilised, Rommel took command of a rifle company in the 13th Infantry Regiment in Stuttgart, a post he held until 1929. In the seclusion of army life and removed from any political involvement, this quiet and humble man lived on his memories of the Great War, memories of comradeship, victory and personal achievements. In 1927 he revisited the battlefields of the Isonzo and Piave, the sites of his heroic feats, accompanied by his wife, Lucie, whom he had married during the war.

The world outside the barracks gate was none of Rommel's concern. In this he was in complete agreement with the way the Reichswehr saw itself. According to the army leadership, political discussions were not permitted. General Hans von Seeckt, commander of the Reichswehr, maintained an icy distance from party squabbles and strove to maintain the Prussian military tradition of a disciplined, apolitical army. Seeckt wrote to his officer corps in his first Order of the Day in April 1920 that political debates within the Reichswehr were incompatible with both the spirit of comradeship and discipline, and could only damage military training. Of course this rhetoric concealed the belief that the present regime, which tore the epaulettes from the shoulders of the officers in 1918, was not the German soldier's true state.

Captain Rommel also drew lessons from the lost Great War. As his experience had been strictly limited to the battlefield and the barracks, these were purely military lessons. One had constructed a military dogma down to the tiniest detail, he wrote, and had held this 'to be the epitome of all military wisdom'. 'Despite the value of strong ties of tradition to the soldierly ethic, it is up to the military leadership to reject these, as in our time military leaders must develop new methods and thereby make others obsolete, as possibilities in war leadership are constantly being changed by technical progress'.[15] According to Rommel the tendency of the aristocratic officer corps to cling to old-fashioned thinking about army organisation blocked an up-to-date understanding of the experiences of the Great War.

In general Rommel was disturbed by the dominant role of the nobility in the officer corps. He believed officers of this class often gained general staff positions as their birthright rather than any accomplishments on the battlefield. To Rommel's way of thinking, the privileges of the nobility sapped the motivation of the average soldier or middle-class officer since the highest rungs on the military career ladder were denied to them. This was counterproductive since modern warfare depended on each individual. Only the seamless co-operation between leader and led could bring about success. Rommel was convinced that social mobility, which had not existed in the Great War, was necessary to foster this co-operation. That is why Rommel laid partial blame for the defeat in the Great War and the supposed treachery of the 'home front' on the aristocracy. After all, the aristocracy succeeded in transferring their privileges from the Kaiser's army to the army of the Republic – every fourth member of the Reichswehr was a nobleman. He was appropriately disapproving of these circles of privilege, a disapproval that found repeated expression in his thirty-year-long correspondence with his wife.

Rommel assumed, like many of his comrades-in-arms, that they would get their revenge some time in the future. This was understandable in that the officer corps' belief was grounded in the perception that war meant the absence of politics. These men accepted war as legitimate, particularly when it came to securing the future of the nation. Germany had lost one seventh of its sovereign territory and numerous colonies and had suffered massive interference with its economy. More importantly, Germany had been utterly humiliated by the terms of the dictated peace. With this in mind, it made it easier for the younger, non-aristocratic officers of the Great War later to bring their opinions closer to Hitler's. In the conclusion to his book, *Infantry Attacks*, Rommel wrote about the obligation that arose from the First World War. Sounding like an appeal, he wrote that, 'the German soldiers who adhered to the path of loyal fulfilment of duty to home and country to the bitter end, [admonish] us survivors and future generations not to fail them when it becomes necessary to make sacrifices for Germany'.[16]

The Coming-Together

As Hitler and his Nazi Party strove for power in the early 1930s, Captain Rommel served as a tactical instructor at the Dresden Infantry School. From this vantage point, removed from politics, he saw his prejudices against the hated political parties and the governments that they formed reaffirmed. They were proving themselves incapable of responding to the great challenges of the time, the global economic crisis and massive unemployment. The polarisation of politics was once again ripping open deep divisions in society, as it had done before in the aftermath of 1918. Increasingly bloody confrontations between the Nazis and Communists already seemed to presage the nightmare of civil war. Seeckt's army had long since slipped away from 'the Republic'. The increasingly isolated and partly conscientiously anti-army Social Democratic Party only barely tolerated the government of Heinrich Brüning, a Chancellor who ruled by presidential decree. This moved the army to the right of the political spectrum. The Hundred Thousand Man Army, and its much-admired old Field Marshal of the Great War, President Paul von Hindenburg, did not believe they were strong enough 'to uphold constitutional law against the National Socialists and Communists, and to protect the borders', as was indicated in an army study.[17] As a result of deep, dark intrigues, the duped and aged President and the Reichswehr leadership decided to try to carry on with a 'boxed-in' Hitler, the Austrian corporal they held in contempt.

24

Hitler's announcement, after power had been handed over to him, that he intended to establish an 'authoritarian state leadership', to eliminate the 'cancer of democracy' and to eradicate Marxism 'root and branch' was met with unrestrained approval by the army. The army was particularly pleased with Hitler's renewed and strengthened intent to revise the Treaty of Versailles and return the Reich to the size it had been before the humiliation of 1918. This revisionist policy would require the rearmament of Germany. To the applause of military leaders (including Reichswehr Minister Walter von Blomberg, who had sympathised with Hitler from the beginning), Hitler declared emphatically as early as 3 February 1933 that it was his deepest desire to return the army to its rightful place of honour in the state. He promised the army and the navy that they would be able to work on the development of the German Reich's military strength with increased resources and without constraint. The *Volkischer Beobachter*[18] reported the position of the Reichswehr Ministry Chief, Colonel Walter von Reichenau when it quoted him as saying, 'Never before has the Wehrmacht been identified more closely with the purposes of the state.' Hitler found his entrée into the Wehrmacht with von Reichenau and von Blomberg. They in turn saw in the corporal from the Great War and his associates nothing more than the leaders of a mass movement. They were willing to support those leaders and thought to regain a position of power for the army and the country.

The Reichswehr leadership therefore totally approved of the propaganda spectacle in the Potsdam Garrison Church, shrine of the Prussian-German army, where Hitler and Hindenburg shook hands beside the resting-place of Frederick the Great. As much as this symbolic act must have meant to the officers who thought they had 'hired' Hitler to be a gesture of subjugation, it meant even more to a broad section of the population as a whole. To them, and to non-aristocratic officers like Rommel, it symbolised much more the union of Imperial and National Socialist Germany. Since they did not know of Hitler's ultimate goals, they were as misled as the philosopher of history Oswald Spengler, who described the 'national coup' as 'something colossal', something enduring in his book, *The Hour of Decision: Germany and World Historical Evolution* published in August 1933. He continued: 'It was Prussian through and through, like the emergence of 1914, which transformed souls in the blink of an eye.'[19] As evidence shows, the enthusiasm of the military for Hitler was widespread, even amongst those officers who later conspired against him. They saw him as the vanquisher of the discord that had traumatised German society since 1918. They believed that each new chapter of national history must begin with a baptism of fire. Therefore the Reichswehr welcomed the terror against Social Democrats and Communists, from whose ranks came the Dutchman named Marinus van der Lubbe who had just burnt down the Reichstag. Thus they could overlook the excesses committed against the Jews. They persuaded themselves that the rapid and forceful demands to 'toe the line' were expressions of common national thought. Very few were worried that Hitler, empowered and authorised by the bourgeois populist parties, might be 'knocked off his stride'. After all, President Hindenburg, and even more importantly, the army itself, was there to control him.

For the army, life seemed to be getting better. Hitler quickly started to act upon his declared intent to rearm. He began by quadrupling the Reichswehr's strength. First he had earmarked funds in the Budget for the expansion. Then he had left the negotiating table at the Geneva Rearmament Conference and pointedly withdrew from the League of Nations in October 1933. The expansion finally improved the promotion chances of officers who had little hope of advancement in the Hundred Thousand Man Army – for example, Rommel had remained a captain for fourteen years. And for the officers from the middle class there was the additional hope that Hitler would eradicate the privileges of the aristocrats. After all, who was better suited to negotiate and modernise antiquated customs than the new Reich Chancellor, a simple corporal from the Great War who continually declared his desire to reconcile Nationalism and Socialism.

Hitler might have had even more enthusiastic support had he not moved in a milieu that many officers rejected. The 'party bigwigs' and their pseudo-military organisations did not impress even the enthusiastic Rommel as 'very trustworthy.' He once wrote his wife that he considered it a 'tragedy' that Hitler surrounded himself with such people.[20] For the Reichswehr the most important factor was the rise of the proletarian Sturm Abteilung (SA) as a dangerous competitor. Since becoming head of the SA in 1931, Ernst Röhm had transformed the band of political thugs into an organisation of approximately one and a half million men. Within just a few months of the handover of power the Brownshirts were already getting restive, believing that the Junkers, capitalists and generals were being favoured and that they had been handed a raw deal. Röhm therefore wanted a 'second revolution' after which the SA would become the 'true National Army' of the Third Reich, the 'School of the Nation'.

Blomberg and Reichenau feared that the Party's 'Brown Army' would usurp the rightful place of the Wehrmacht (the new name of the Reichswehr). They began a concentrated effort to get Hitler to favour the 'rightful' army. In addition they systematically undermined the position of the army commander, General Kurt Freiherr von Hammerstein-Equord, a critic of the Nazis, and forced his resignation in the autumn of 1933. Early in 1934 von Blomberg ordered the introduction of the Nazi emblem as the official symbol of the armed forces, and later adopted the 'Aryan regulation', which had been used to remove Jews from the civil service.

As Röhm did not give in, Hitler found himself caught between the leader of the Brownshirts and the conservative camp, where displeasure was growing. Ever the gambler, Hitler placed his bets on the Wehrmacht in the summer of 1934 because he realised that only it had the competence to achieve his dreams of expansion. With the help of the SS and backing from the armed forces he delivered a decapitating stroke against the SA leadership. However, Hitler did not content himself with liquidating Röhm and other SA leaders. He also ordered the murder of opponents in the conservative camp, including the former Chancellor General Kurt von Schleicher and other officers. Ignoring the fact that they were accomplices in Hitler's murderous actions, the Wehrmacht leadership surrounding von Blomberg, and in fact the entire German public, literally celebrated the massacre. For them the Führer seemed to have finally rid himself of the dark, frightening players in the national political game. Even Rommel dearly wanted to believe the propaganda spread by Joseph Goebbels, that Röhm and the others were conspiring with foreign powers and had merely received their just desserts. Nevertheless he thought Hitler had gone too far. He said to his adjutant at the time, 'The Führer should not have

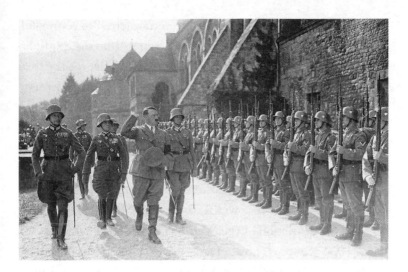

Purely formal. First meeting with Hitler in Goslar, September 1934.

done that. He is not aware of his power, otherwise he would have used it more generously and legitimately.'[21]

When Hindenburg died a few weeks later and the offices of Chancellor and President were combined, Rommel did not hesitate to follow von Blomberg's orders to swear loyalty to Hitler. While it is true that he most likely attached no great importance to taking the oath, his willingness probably stemmed as much from his openness to change as from the fact that he and his fellow officers had remained 'Children of the Imperial Era'. These 'Children' needed an 'ersatz' monarch, a powerful leader. This need for strong political authority – despite their recognition of the shortcomings of the nobility's previous leadership – created one of the cornerstones of the officer corps' ties to Hitler.

The zealous Rommel was drawn early on into the proximity of the man who now had the fate of the Reich in his hands. In early October 1933, Rommel had been transferred to command the Goslar Rifle Battalion. He stepped squarely into the spotlight in late September 1934 when he was to meet Hitler for the first time. The original plans for the parade at the Reichsbauerntag put the SS contingent in front of Rommel's Rifle Battalion since they were responsible for the Führer's security. Rommel declared that his battalion would not turn out under these circumstances. He got his way and the SS stayed in the background. His actual meeting with Hitler was, of course, purely formal – a military salute, handshake, a few words about the Pour-le-Mérite, and then a joint inspection of the Wehrmacht honour guard.

In 1935 Rommel, now a Lieutenant-Colonel, was posted to the Potsdam War College as Tactics Instructor. That same year Hitler introduced compulsory military service in direct contravention of the Treaty of Versailles. He forced the measure past a vacillating Wehrmacht leadership, and announced it on state radio on 15 March. At the same time he announced that he planned to raise troop strength to 550,000. The enthusiasm of the people, including Rommel, was overwhelming. In one stroke Hitler had managed to restore the self-respect of the German people. No longer did they (and in particular, the veterans of the Front) have to suffer the trauma of 1918/19. It was no wonder then that the 44-year-old Rommel considered his temporary assignment to Hitler's personal protection command as a great honour. He was responsible for Hitler's security at the Nuremberg Rally in late summer 1936, shortly after the Olympic Games in Berlin. Apparently Rommel's uncompromisingly thorough execution of his assignment brought the ambitious Lieutenant-Colonel to Hitler's attention. Hitler supposedly requested Rommel's presence on the evening of the event so he could thank him personally.

Unlike Rommel, who increasingly admired Hitler's decisiveness, the Wehrmacht leadership was less and less comfortable with the Führer's leadership. A case in point was their disquiet before and during the occupation of the Rhineland in March 1936. Both the Commander-in-Chief of the Army, Field Marshal Walter von Fritsch, and Reichswehr Minister von Blomberg had initially raised doubts about it, and later urgently warned against the action. Hitler ignored their reservations and dared to take a bold course. Events seemed to prove him right when the western powers did not intervene. He took the opportunity to lecture the generals about his superiority. The result was no different when Hitler chose to support Franco's Nationalists during the Spanish Civil War. Rommel looked down on the 'Doubting Thomases'. Later he wrote his wife, 'I was a witness to a great speech to our military commanders and their superiors. The Führer spoke very bluntly. But then this seems necessary, as when one speaks with a group of comrades there is seldom a single one who participates with whole-hearted conviction.'[22]

Rommel was unaware that Hitler had openly outlined his goals to the Wehrmacht leadership in early November 1937. He had declared he had made an 'unalterable decision' to launch a campaign against Stalin's Soviet Union no later than 1943/45 to finally 'solve the question of German territory' and that such a campaign might make a war with his preferred ally Great Britain no longer an impossibility.[23] His mad, even 'lunatic', plans startled von Blomberg and the Wehrmacht leadership. But they did not object again; they had had enough of Hitler's lectures. Nevertheless they continued to drag their feet. This hesitancy undermined their authority with up-and-coming junior officers and this, with the gradually increasing influence of the Reichsführer-SS Heinrich Himmler, sealed their fate.

Personnel changes at the top of the Wehrmacht became necessary when it was revealed that von Blomberg's new bride had once worked as a prostitute, and that a stable lad had accused von Fritsch of homosexuality. Hitler appointed Walter von Brauchitsch Commander-in-Chief of the Army, who had paved the way for his appointment by promising that he would spare no effort in bringing the Army closer to the State and its *Weltanschauung*. Additionally he allowed far-reaching personnel and administrative changes in the Wehrmacht, which gave Hitler immediate command of the Wehrmacht from then on. He created a High Command of the Armed Forces (Oberkommando der Wehrmacht – OKW), essentially his own staff, and put it into direct competition with the High Command of the Army (Oberkommando des Heeres – OKH). He appointed Wilhelm Keitel Chief of the OKW, a man whom Ulrich von Hassell (later executed as one of the plotters against Hitler) had deemed 'totally lacking in judgement' and to whom he attributed an almost 'subservient attitude toward the party'.[24] Even his grateful Führer once described him as 'a man with the brains of a theatre doorman'.[25] The intelligent Alfred Jodl became OKW Chief of Staff.

Hitler gained unfettered control of the Wehrmacht with this coup. It lost what independence it had, and became a tool in his hands. A few weeks later he ordered the invasion of his Austrian homeland, where the Wehrmacht and its Supreme Commander were greeted enthusiastically by the vast majority of the population. Rommel's potential rise to high rank was made possible by the removal of the old Wehrmacht leadership. He noted, from a speech by Hitler at the time, 'the German

Wehrmacht is the sword of the new German Weltanschauung'[26] – a Weltanschauung whose worth from Rommel's perspective lay solely in its usefulness for the military.

It is possible that by this time Hitler had become familiar with Rommel's name through reading his book *Infantry Attacks*, which had been published in 1937 by the Potsdam publisher Voggenreiter. Hitler was supposed to have been impressed by the battle descriptions from the Great War. Apparently the material in the book, which became a best-seller, transported him back to those never-to-be-forgotten years. Hitler's Luftwaffe adjutant, Nicolas von Below, was also able to give the Führer a first-hand account of Rommel's tactical abilities, as he had been a student of Rommel's at the Dresden War College, and had the utmost respect for his teachings. Below repeatedly pointed out the Swabian Rommel to the Reich Chancellor when asked about 'competent front line officers who had no previous general staff experience'.[27]

And so it came about that Rommel, who had participated in a few Nazi training courses of a couple of days' duration for higher-level Wehrmacht officers, was enlisted by Hitler for special assignments, with gradually increasing frequency. In early October 1938, shortly after the Munich Agreement, he was installed as commander of the Führer's personal escort battalion. From this position he saw how the people cheered Hitler during the occupation of the Sudetenland. His personal involvement in and observation of these historic events brought him closer to Hitler. In December 1938 Hitler gave him a personally-autographed photograph in a silver frame as a souvenir of those historic moments. Rommel is supposed to have put this on the list of 'most important things' he wanted to be sure his wife had removed to safety in the event of an air raid.

Rommel's next assignment after his tour of duty as commander of the Führer's escort battalion was as Commander of the War College in Wiener Neustadt. His credentials as a brilliant tactician at the Infantry School in Potsdam made him a natural choice for the head of what was supposed to become the most modern war college in Europe. Hitler believed Rommel had all the attributes to be the ideal candidate for the position. He was ambitious, he hungered for responsibility, he had proven tactical capabilities and knowledge, and most of all, he was a hero of the Great War. Rommel felt flattered by the choice and was grateful for the trust placed in him.

In March 1939 Hitler temporarily relieved Rommel of his post at Wiener Neustadt, assigning him once again the command of the Führer Headquarters, this time during the invasion of the so-called 'Rest-Tschechei', the remaining territory of Czechoslovakia. And once again an eager Rommel teamed up with an intrepid Führer. Hitler had arrived at the Czech border without a personal guard, but Rommel urged him to proceed directly to the Hradschin, the Prague Castle, under his protection. The horrified generals, and Himmler, who were with him, objected. However, Rommel persuaded Hitler. 'You have no other choice. For you, my Führer, there is only the path into the heart of the country, into the capital, and up to the Castle of Prague.' Hitler allowed himself to be convinced and drove on. 'He never . . . forgot that I gave him this advice,' Rommel later proudly boasted.[28] Newsreels showed Hitler and Rommel driving side-by-side up to Prague Castle.

As Rommel spent more time with Hitler, and got to know him better, he believed he recognised traits they had in common. He equated his courage and determination as a First Lieutenant in the Great War when he led his troops in battle with Hitler's taking the fate of the Reich in his own hands. Hitler had, as he had boldly proclaimed years earlier, burst the shackles of the Treaty of Versailles and even brought the 'Ostmark' (Austria) and the German-speaking border territories 'home into the Reich'. The 'old dream' of a greater German nation-state had become a reality.

In Rommel's eyes the man who had made this dream a reality really just wanted to be the First Soldier of the German Reich. This view was strengthened when Rommel saw daily life in the Führer Headquarters during his assignments there. Money and property seemed to hold no value for Hitler. He also seemed to be above other temptations. In this first phase of his revisionist politics, which coincided with his world-shattering political dreams, he was so driven that he once said he would not be on earth for pleasure. Conditions were appropriately spartan at the Führer Headquarters. The furniture was simple, functional and reduced to the bare minimum, just a wardrobe, a table, a chair and a cot. For meals the vegetarian Hitler ate typical soldier's rations: stews that the troops ate (often pearl barley soup with hard bread) and mineral water to drink. On journeys he carried his essential personal effects in a small suit-case. Rommel was impressed by Hitler's apparent adherence to the principle 'service before self' because it reflected his own modest style in his personal life as a soldier.

Rommel soon realised that he agreed with Hitler on the main focus of rearmament. The Commander-in-Chief was insistent on motorising the Army and rapidly developing an operationally-ready air and tank force. Both men found themselves at odds with many in the General Staff on this issue, who favoured the build-up of heavy artillery, engi-neers, railroad troops and intelligence. Like Rommel, Hitler strongly favoured the tank as the decisive weapon in modern land warfare.

Rommel and Hitler also had many other things in common, such as their mutual admiration for Napoleon. Hitler had thoroughly absorbed the Nazi's Philipp Bouhler's biography of Napoleon, *Kometenpfad eines Genies*, and liked to quote the Corsican's motto, 'Activité, activité, vitesse!' When the Wehrmacht had overrun France, Hitler spent a long time at Napoleon's sarcophagus at Les Invalides in Paris. Shortly thereafter he arranged for the remains of Napoleon's son, the Duke of Reichstadt, to be exhumed from the Imperial Crypt in Vienna and moved to Paris so he could be laid to rest next to his father. This act was also a political gesture to Vichy France, which Hitler wanted to incorporate into his continental European front against Great Britain. As a young soldier Rommel had already acquired an engraving showing the exiled Napoleon gazing across the ocean from St. Helena. He particularly admired the Emperor's style of leadership, especially his saying that you could not command the Grande Armée from the Tuileries. In other words Napoleon preferred to lead from the front, as Rommel did when he was a company commander in the Great War.

In the last days before the Second World War, Hitler promoted Colonel Rommel to Major-General, retroactive to 1 June 1939. When the war started shortly thereafter with the German invasion of Poland and the subsequent declarations of war by France and Great Britain, Rommel, like his Supreme Commander, saw the day of reckoning approaching for the debacle of 1914–18. He wrote to his wife: 'isn't it wonderful that we have this man?'[29] Rommel's impression was that a 'magnetic, maybe hypnotic, strength' emanated from him, 'which had its deepest origin in the belief that he was called upon

36

by God or Providence to lead the German people "upwards to the sun"'. At times he would speak 'from the depths of his being. . . like a prophet'.[30] Accordingly he was deeply shattered when the cabinetmaker from Königsbrunn, Georg Elser, attempted to assassinate Hitler at the beginning of November 1939. 'It is inconceivable if the attempt had succeeded.'[31]

In his assignment as commander of the Führer's Headquarters Rommel had the opportunity to keep in close personal contact with his Supreme Commander on a daily basis. This lasted for almost half a year starting in August 1939. Visitors to Headquarters during that time claimed to sense 'an atmosphere of servility, nervousness and embarrassment', but Rommel had no such impression, since he had come to see Hitler as a demi-god. He was flattered when Hitler took time to chat with him. It was a particular honour for the General to be included in the 'most intimate meetings'. This inclusion meant more to him than his rank as general. Hitler's 'astounding gift . . . to imme-diately grasp the critical points and derive solutions from them in all meetings' fascinated Rommel. And then there was Hitler's courage. 'I had a lot of trouble with him', he reported at the time of the Polish campaign. 'He always wanted to be with the advance units. It seemed to give him pleasure to be under fire.'[32]

Soon after his posting Rommel was even able to savour the occasional honour of sitting next to Hitler at lunch, an honour that he specifically mentioned in letters to his wife. He recorded every new mark of favour from Hitler precisely: 'Was allowed to chat for almost two hours with him about military problems yesterday. He is extraordinarily friendly toward me'.[33] It was hardly surprising therefore that Rommel was soon allowed to be present at the regular evening 'situation conferences' during the Polish campaign (a campaign where modern tank tactics celebrated their first triumphs) and 'occasionally even to speak a word', as he enthusiastically reported to his wife.[34]

Rommel responded to all this recognition with unswerving loyalty. On one of the Führer's many trips to the front during the Polish campaign Rommel even snubbed the powerful Martin Bormann, the future head of the Party Chancellery. As Bormann's car tried to fall into line behind Hitler's vehicle on the way to the conquered port of Gdingen, Rommel stepped squarely into the road and rebuked the party functionary with the words, 'I am the commander of the Führer's Headquarters. This is no kindergarten excursion. You will do as I say.'[35] Walter Warlimont, Deputy Wehrmacht Chief of Staff, who was an eyewitness, later wrote about Bormann's reaction. He responded with 'furious screams' and 'swore [at Rommel] in an outrageous manner'. Warlimont 'expressed his outrage about Bormann's behaviour at this point', and wrote that 'Rommel . . . requested that Schmundt, the Wehrmacht Chief Adjutant, be informed of the incident'.[36] Warlimont made his report and Schmundt, Rommel's friend, reported it to Hitler in turn. Bormann never forgot nor forgave the incident. Hitler, on the other hand, was enthusiastic about Rommel. He liked his total devotion, as well as his military expertise, courage and determination. Rommel, in turn, could now believe that the 'soldier was worth something again' after the humiliation of losing the First World War. The schoolmaster's son from the small Swabian town of Heidenheim had managed to achieve recognition as a soldier. He had moved up into Hitler's immediate circle and enjoyed the favour of the man who was preparing to raise Germany to superpower status, the man 'who knows what is best for us'. Rommel was totally under the spell of his supreme commander; he had become the 'Führer's General'.

Proud to be part of it. On Hitler's special train with Himmler and Schmundt, 1939.

Rommel was so blinded by his rapid rise in Hitler's favour that he did not see Nazism's underlying contempt for mankind, nor did he make any effort to see its 'true face'. From his perspective as a serving soldier the political leadership and the Wehrmacht were two entirely different things. He restricted himself, as did most of his fellow generals, to purely military matters. The dark side of Nazism did not seem, on balance, to be as important as what Hitler was doing for Germany. Just how much Rommel deluded himself that Hitler's war was not just for the benefit of the Germans is apparent in a letter he wrote to his wife from occupied Warsaw in early October 1939. 'About every tenth house is burned out and collapsed. There are no more shops. The shop windows are shattered; the owners have boarded them up. There has been no water, no light, no gas and no food for two days now . . . The Lord Mayor is estimating 40,000 dead and wounded.' Rommel's conclusion was frighteningly naïve, 'The inhabitants draw a breath of relief that we have arrived and rescued them.'[37]

Just how little Rommel the soldier was concerned with National Socialist politics was demonstrated by the way he ignored such displays as Hitler's endless rabble-rousing tirades against all things Jewish, the Nurmberg Race Laws, and even 'Crystal Night'. This lack of concern is even more remarkable since he attended National Socialism courses where he would have been exposed to the insane concept of the final battle between the Aryan and the Jewish people. Rommel had heard Himmler say on one occasion that the next decades would not bring a debate on foreign policy, 'but rather they required the fight to exterminate all the world's subhuman opponents of Germany as the core nation of the Nordic race . . .'.[38]

The reports spread about Rommel after the Second World War sound rather naïve; that he only found out about the mass murders in the East very late is highly unlikely. As a matter of fact, as commander of the Führer's Headquarters during the Polish campaign he was not on the spot where the SS task-forces were liquidating Jews and other 'racially inferior' people in their hundreds of thousands, but he must have known, just as the generals of the High Command of the Wehrmacht knew – the same generals who at first tried to avoid responsibility, but fairly rapidly degraded themselves into accomplices in Hitler's racist war of extermination. It was reported that in 1943 Rommel suggested to Hitler that Germany would be better off if a Jew could become a Gauleiter. Hitler is then supposed to have responded, 'My dear Rommel, you have understood nothing of what I want'.[39] Hitler would have been absolutely in character if his general had actually suggested this and he had responded in this way.

No matter how much Rommel might have ignored Nazi policy and the crimes committed in its furtherance, he was

'The population is relieved that we've come . . .'. With Hitler in Warsaw, September 1939.

personally concerned that the traditional military ethos of the German army would be upheld in the modern armed forces of National Socialist Germany. His later service in North Africa and France made it easier for him to distance himself from Hitler's racist war in the East. For example, when he received the order to 'liquidate on the spot' Free French prisoners who had been fighting on the side of the British on the spurious reason that they were partisans under international law, he simply burned it. He did not 'separate out' Jews, any more than he entertained requests that white soldiers be separated from coloureds in prison camps. He justified this decision on the basis that since these coloured men had fought side-by-side with their white comrades they would all have to carry the burden of captivity together. Rommel satisfied himself with the fact that he and his command would act decently. He did

41

not question the moral calibre of the order's sender – Hitler. Perhaps he comforted himself, as did many of Hitler's supporters, by separating the man and the party. The 'Führer' represented everything good about the New Germany; the 'Party big shots' were responsible for everything bad.

Advancement

Hitler's successes at the beginning of the Second World War fascinated Rommel and drew him more and more under his spell. After the invasion of Poland Denmark was occupied, then the British were pre-empted in Norway. Then the Supreme Commander adopted a battle plan to attack France that was bolder than anything previously thought of. In the First World War the Germans had attacked in a broad arc through the Belgian plains. This time the tanks and motorised units of the Wehrmacht would attack through the rough terrain of the Ardennes, a course of action no one thought possible. Rommel was proud, as were millions of his German compatriots, to follow a man who seemed to have such a comprehensive grasp of modern battle tactics. In April 1940 he wrote, 'Well, if we didn't have the Führer, I don't know whether there would be another German who so brilliantly masters the art of military and political leadership in equal measure.'[40]

Contrary to millions of others Rommel was chosen as one of the inner circle of Hitler's favourites. Therefore it should have come as no surprise to the resentful members of the General Staff when Hitler gave Rommel (whom they despised as a 'parvenu') a prime command. Rommel, as a 'modern-thinking general', was given a unit with the most up-to-date equipment to allow him to take part in Hitler's daredevil plan for the invasion of France. Previously the Chief of Army Personnel had denied Rommel's request for a similar assignment, and recommended the experienced First World War infantry veteran for command of a mountain division. Rommel saw it as the crowning achievement of his career to date when Hitler overruled his personnel chief and gave him command of the 7th Panzer Division, stationed at Bad Godesberg. When Rommel left the Führer's Headquarters Hitler gave him a copy of *Mein Kampf* with a personal dedication. He had inscribed it, 'General Rommel – with friendly memories'.[41]

In May 1940, after weeks of training in the Wahner Heide near Cologne, Rommel headed west for the second time of his life, now commanding the division that was the spearhead of the Fourth Army. Before moving out he wrote his wife, 'In half an hour we will actually be departing here. By the time this letter arrives you will already be aware of what is in play. Don't worry yourself. Everything has gone well to date and it will be all right . . . At dusk we will set off. How long we have waited for this.'[42] After only two weeks his tanks had broken through the French defences. Cambrai, Arras, Lille and Sotteville were phases in his lightning advance before he reached the sea at Dieppe on 10 June. More than 10,000 French and British soldiers surrendered to him at Saint-Valéry and Cherbourg. Hitler was full of enthusiasm for his general.

France surrendered in mid-June. By Hitler's order they assembled in the same railway carriage in the forest of Compiègne in which the Centre Party politician Erzberger had signed the 'humiliating ceasefire' in 1918, only this time the roles were reversed. Hitler had risen to the peak of his power. The pictures of his self-satisfied gleeful gestures outside the carriage bear powerful witness to this. Not only for him, but also for Rommel (the first divisional commander to be decorated with the Knight's Cross of the Iron Cross in the Western Campaign), victory was final proof of the new order's superiority over the 'decadent' western democracies, as well as Imperial Germany and the Weimar Republic. For four long years German armies had bled to death in their battle against the 'arch enemy' in the First World War. Hitler's campaign, in comparison, took only six weeks, with relatively few losses.

'The greatest military leader of all time.' Kluge, Rommel, Hitler during the Western Campaign.

The success of these campaigns had two results, which fatally reinforced each other. First, Hitler believed that Russia could be overwhelmed equally quickly; after all, they had been defeated in the First World War. Second, his generals and the overwhelming majority of the German people saw Hitler, in the words of the Chief of Staff of the OKW Keitel, as 'the greatest commander of all time', and would now blindly follow his 'strategic genius'.

Rommel's ties to Hitler were also strengthened after the victory in the West. Up to then he had only been able to distinguish himself through his security assignments. In France he had now been able to demonstrate his true military capabilities as a divisional commander. He had eagerly tried to justify the confidence placed in him. To get his merits noticed by Hitler he drafted an interim report three weeks after the start of the Western Campaign. He sent off a detailed report of the losses his unit had inflicted on the enemy. At the end of the Western Campaign he once again brought himself to Hitler's attention. He had put together a carefully-prepared, though in some places 'enhanced', history of his division. The report was 'enhanced' by claiming other tank regiments' successes to bolster his own image. Naturally there were protests. One colonel, whom Rommel later had relieved of command in Africa, complained to the OKH. Since Rommel's self-promotion did not sit well with the High Command, Halder, the Chief of the General Staff, refused to release official photographs that Rommel had requested for preparation of the history in book form.

Hitler received this assessment of the French campaign shortly after Christmas 1940 by way of Rommel's 'back channel', the Führer's senior Wehrmacht Adjutant Rudolph Schmundt, who would be named Chief of Army Personnel in the summer of 1942. Schmundt and Rommel had a deep mutual regard, which grew into an increasing friendship. Schmundt was also an admirer of Hitler. 'What greatness! What an idealist! What joy to serve such a leader!' he once said.[43] Like Rommel, he also held Hitler's inner circle in contempt. 'Yes, unfortunately the Führer is surrounded by a bunch of scoundrels. But most of these party bulls are remnants from the old days, from the movement's time of struggle'.[44] Schmundt enjoyed Hitler's esteem, and had a certain amount of influence. Rommel placed great value on their friendship since he could use it to gain direct contact with Hitler when he felt it important, thus bypassing the increasingly resentful General Staff officers from the OKW and OKH.

It was Schmundt who informed Rommel of Hitler's reaction to the manuscript history. 'I was able to present your ever so clearly compiled history of your division to the Führer while still at the Berghof . . .! You can imagine with what joy the Führer studied it'. 'You can be proud of what you have achieved,' Hitler wrote Rommel on 20 December 1940,[45] expressing his pleasure and goodwill to Rommel at the same time. Mixed in with Rommel's 'unending pride that the Führer, despite all the work weighing him down, had found the time to concern himself with my history and write to me'[46] was the hope that Hitler would soon select him for a higher, more important command.

Rommel's hopes had already been fulfilled by the time Hitler praised him to the Wehrmacht leadership on 3 February 1941 as an 'unbelievably tough commander who lead his Panzer division in France like a reconnaissance party and advanced to the Channel coast without regard for danger or physical exhaustion.' The general was supposed to sort out the serious situation in North Africa where the British were threatening to drive Italy out of its North African colony, Tripolitania. When Hitler chose Rommel he was once again disregarding the recommendation of the army leadership. Halder had chosen General Hans Freiherr von Funck, a classic example of the Prussian officer corps, for the assignment. Hitler did not trust von Funck and thought him too pessimistic. In Hitler's opinion the situation called for the unconventional tactics and perpetual optimism of Rommel, whom he had promoted to Lieutenant-General in January 1941. Hitler once justified his decision to an Italian diplomat with the view that Rommel had the capability to 'carry away his troops, which is an absolute essential for an army leader of a unit which has to fight under particularly difficult environmental conditions such as in North Africa.'[47] In a letter, Hitler announced to his 'Axis Partner' Benito Mussolini that he would put 'the boldest *Panzerwaffen* general that we have in the German army' at the head of the German intervention corps required for the defence of Tripolitania.[48] Hitler had personally briefed Rommel on his assignment on 6 February 1941, just a year after he had been given command of the 7th Panzer Division. He knew how to flatter Rommel, for he told him that he was the one man who would be able to adapt to the completely different conditions of the 'African Theatre' faster then anyone else. Rommel recounted this in a letter to his wife, and later told her in another letter that Hitler had named his unit the German Afrika Korps in deference to his earlier service in the German Alpine Corps. With this move Hitler deftly combined the traditions of the old and the new Germany. It was also a dig at his military ally who had failed against Great Britain and Greece, since the Alpine Corps had fought successfully against the Italians in the First World War.

The marks of favour were not yet sufficient. Hitler ordered his senior army adjutant to accompany Rommel during his first days in Africa. On 12 February 1941 they both set foot on African soil for the first time. One event shortly after their arrival indicates how favourably disposed Hitler was to Rommel. The new commander of the Afrika Korps saw the opportunity for some early successes. However, the North African theatre was a coalition and Rommel was formally under the Italian Supreme Command. From the start, even

47

On the way to the 'Führer'. Rommel at the 'Wolfsschanze' in July 1941.

before his units had arrived, he was worried that his Italian ally would claim credit for his hard-won victories. He wanted to get assurance through Schmundt that he would be credited with his successes when they came. A few days after he returned from Africa Schmundt was able to consult with Hitler, and subsequently reassured Rommel with the message, 'It has been confirmed with the Führer that an historic distortion of contributions will not take place anymore.'[49]

Rommel's worries resulted from some negative experiences in the First World War, when other men had been decorated for taking important enemy positions that Rommel had actually taken. This had affected the young officer so deeply that even though the Kaiser eventually awarded him the Pour-le-Mérite after the battle of Longarone in December 1917, he forced the Reich Archive to print a self-serving 14-page supplement.

While the war was still in progress he submitted a formal written complaint based on his personal notes in which he claimed entitlement to the decorations bestowed on others, but he received no response from the commander of the Alpine Corps. After the war he demanded the army historians correct the official historical record in his favour.

Schmundt, to whom Rommel had given a long list of requirements when he returned to Germany, wrote to the 'greatly to be admired general' that Hitler (at the Berghof) was already 'feverishly awaiting' news from the North African war zone and was 'totally concentrated on the Libyan theatre of war.' As to the wish list, Schmundt responded, 'all wishes will be enforced by me by authority of the Führer'.[50] At the end of March the 'greatly admired general' resumed his attacks, taking El Agheila, Marsa el Brega and Benghazi, surrounding Tobruk and advancing to the Egyptian border near Sollum by June.

However, Rommel's successes were soon impeded by an unexpected problem. Hitler became focussed on the coming Russian campaign and North Africa receded into secondary importance. The build up for the imminent Eastern Campaign required enormous commitments in supplies and troops, so he could spare relatively little for Rommel. Moreover, as the war would not be successfully completed in a matter of a few weeks as anticipated, this situation would not improve. The North African campaign needed to slow down for a while; consequently Rommel's fortunes of war rose and fell in 1941 and 1942.

During this period, however, Rommel's personal military fortunes were rising to their zenith. Medals, promotions and other marks of Hitler's favour piled up during Rommel's 'African years' in a way no other Wehrmacht general could match. He received the Oak Leaves to the Knight's Cross in

March 1941 for his successes with the 7th Panzer Division on the Western Front. As a welcoming gesture at the Reich Chancellery Hitler had the medal draped around Rommel's neck. Hitler was supposed to have been 'full of praise for this general' and was to have seen the developments in North Africa as 'very positive'.[51] The recapture of Cyrenaica shortly thereafter brought him Hitler's congratulations.

The tank battle at Sollum in mid-June 1941, and the early successes in the East, put Hitler in 'the best of moods.' When he received Rommel at the end of July at the 'Wolfsschanze', the Führer headquarters at Rastenburg in East Prussia, and congratulated him on his victories, there were already hints of his appointment as General of the Panzer Truppe; it was officially announced shortly thereafter. No longer would the General Staff officers who were competing with him for Hitler's favour have the ability to hinder his climb. Hitler still praised him when Rommel had to accept severe military setbacks and the loss of territory in the winter of 1941. He mentioned him in one of his marathon speeches at the beginning of December and insisted on sending Rommel a personal New Year's greeting expressing his confidence and saying, 'I know that I can depend on my Panzer Division in the New Year'.[52] Hitler even expressed his approval of the retreat to Rommel's Chief of Staff. The Führer was full of praise and admiration, he reported on his return to Africa. 'Tell . . . Rommel I admire him.'[53]

Rommel had barely launched his counteroffensive at the end of January 1942, 'firmly believing in the protective and victory giving Hand of God', when he learned of yet another honour. In January 1942 the 'Panzer Division Afrika' became the 'Panzerarmee Afrika', and would include all Italian motorised units at the front. The success of the offensive made the timing

Grateful to be able to serve the 'New Idea'. At the presentation of the 'Swords' to the Knight's Cross, March 1942.

of Rommel's promotion to full General (Generaloberst) perfect, he was the youngest Wehrmacht general ever to have attained this rank. Hitler extended highest praise to him in his 'great speech' as Lucie Rommel wrote to her husband at the end of January. She was 'frightfully proud', as was 'the entire nation, as shown by the storm of applause when the Führer . . . mentioned your name yesterday and spoke of our Generaloberst'.[54] In mid-February Hitler gave another expression of his admiration when he awarded him the Swords to the Oak Leaves of the Knight's Cross. Rommel was only the sixth officer in the Wehrmacht and the first Army officer to receive the decoration. Newsreel pictures show in great detail the Supreme Commander of the Panzerarmee Afrika, his chest swollen with pride, receiving his award. Rommel was grateful to be able to 'work for the Führer, nation and the new idea', as he wrote in a private letter.[55]

At the end of May 1942 (Cyrenaica was back in the hands of the Axis) Rommel resumed the offensive against Tobruk, which he had been forced to discontinue in February. Before the defenders had even surrendered the Commander-in-Chief South, Field Marshal Albert Kesselring, had delivered Hitler's congratulations. Two days after the fall of Tobruk, on 23 June 1942, the German News Bureau reported that Rommel had been promoted to Field Marshal. On the morning of 30 September 1942, at the Reich Chancellery, Hitler presented the field marshal's baton to Rommel. At 50 years of age, he was the youngest Field Marshal in the Wehrmacht. On the same evening Hitler honoured him with a rally for the Fourth Winterhilfswerk in front of Party and Wehrmacht delegations in the Berliner Sportpalast. Millions could listen to it on their Volksempfänger (inexpensive wireless sets). By honouring Rommel, Hitler was using him as an example of the men who represented his vision of the 'next generation of revolutionary officers and generals'. He had youth, imagination and a talent for improvisation. He was one of those 'fellows' who committed himself unconditionally to his goals, fellows whom Hitler regretted not having consistently selected and developed during peacetime. This was particularly true as the Russian campaign dragged on longer and longer. Being able to honour Rommel also gave the event an air of victory, very useful since the summer campaign in Russia was not delivering the expected triumphs.

This was Rommel's fifth promotion since being appointed general shortly before the outbreak of war. He had already received the Knight's Cross, the Oak Leaves and now the Swords. He knew to whom he owed his meteoric rise. 'As I

Elevation to Immortality. The presentation of the Field Marshal's baton, September 1942.

have just found out . . . I owe my latest promotion only to the Führer. You can just imagine my joy over this. His recognition of my achievements is the highest I could wish for myself.' These words, written in a letter home to Swabia, described his pride at a previous promotion.[56] In another letter he said 'it is very nice to attain such heights at my age.' Everything 'was like a dream.'[57] This man, of whom it was said he was a soldier in body and soul during the First World War, had become a Field Marshal and with this an 'immortal'. With his rank came life-long privileges. He would take a permanent place in the military history of the Reich.

By this juncture Hitler was convinced of Erwin Rommel's historic greatness. When his tanks rolled toward the Nile after the capture of Tobruk they seemed unstoppable. Hitler warned a representative of the Foreign Minister Joachim von Ribbentrop that the Foreign Office should not dare 'to send an envoy to Egypt upon the occupation of Alexandria and Cairo. Rommel is a generalissimo so covered in immortal glory and already considered one of the most amazing figures in the history of war that it would be absurd for the Foreign Office to want to interfere in matters there.'[58]

Rommel was still not satisfied with what he had accomplished. His ambition continued to drive him further, and not merely toward Egypt. He wanted to become Commander-in-Chief of the Army. Rumours that Hitler had thought about this move from time to time, to give his 'favourite general' supreme command of the army, had circulated numerous times in the previous year. He had dismissed von Brauchitsch in December 1941 and had not appointed a successor. Rommel's position seemed to solidify after he took Tobruk in June 1942. The naval liaison officer to the OKH reported to the naval leadership that the imminent appointment of the unpopular social climber was considered an 'open secret'. Even Goebbels, whose propaganda had made Rommel into the epitome of the German national hero, lobbied for him. He outlined Rommel's character traits for Hitler, which practically predestined him to assume the command and execute the role in a National Socialist manner. He wrote in his diary that Rommel 'is ideologically sound, is not just sympathetic to the National Socialists. He is a National Socialist; he is a troop leader with a gift for improvisation, personally courageous and extraordinarily inventive. These are the kinds of soldiers we need. Rommel is the coming Supreme Commander of the Army.'[59]

Embittered Opponents.
Rommel and Keitel
at the rally on the
occasion of the 4th
Winterhilfswerk in the
Berliner Sportpalast,
September 1942.

Rommel's constant presence at Führer Headquarters in the spring of 1943 once again supplied new gist for the rumour mill. An entry in one Army officer's diary at that time said, 'Apparently Hitler intends to divide the chiefs of the General Staff. Rommel is supposed to become Supreme Commander z. b. V. [for special purposes].'[60] Rommel himself consciously described the role he was exercising in the daily situation briefings with the words, 'I was there as advisor, in other words as a kind of reigning supreme commander of the Army. That is how it was intended.'[61] Even if he had not been formally appointed, Rommel now saw himself as *de facto* one of Hitler's closest advisers on military matters. He believed this partly because Hitler during those weeks frequently asked his opinion about the latest developments in armoured vehicles. Hitler's favourite, not one of the General Staff, believed he had managed to by-pass this clique, which enervated Hitler with its 'constant doubts', that he had reached the top rung.

Irritations

Hitler's relationship with Rommel began to cool in the autumn of 1942. It was because the tide of war had finally begun to turn against the Reich. Later, in January 1943, an entire Germany army would be annihilated at Stalingrad, which was at the southern end of an Eastern Front that stretched 2,000 kilometres. In North Africa, where the Panzerarmee Afrika had penetrated as far as El Alamein, Allied troops under the command of Lieutenant-General Bernard Montgomery were massing in overwhelming numbers for a decisive counter-offensive.

The first serious difference of opinion between Rommel and Hitler came when Rommel, on his own initiative, ordered his troops to retreat after a British breakthrough on the German-Italian El Alamein front. He had concealed that the retreat was already underway in a radio message to Führer Headquarters with the words: 'consequently the army is preparing to fall back, fighting step by step, in the face of superior enemy pressure as of 3 November [1942]. The infantry divisions will be pulled back during the night of 2–3 November to support this'.[62]

An infuriated Hitler sent the first of what were to become depressingly frequent messages to his commanders; stand your ground. The order said, 'The entire German nation is with me, in faithful confidence in your personal leadership ability and the bravery of the German and Italian troops under your command, in following the heroic defence of Egypt. In your situation there can be no other thought than to wait it out, give no ground, and throw into the battle every weapon and every soldier who can be made available . . . Despite his superiority the enemy will also be at the limits of his strength. It would not be the first time in history that the stronger will triumphs over the stronger battalions of the enemy. You can show your troops no other path than to victory or death. Signed, Adolf Hitler.'[63]

When he received this order Rommel is reputed to have told his officers that if he stood his ground there would be no army in three days. Nevertheless he temporarily broke off the retreat. He sent another radio message on 4 November demanding Hitler rescind the order, and meanwhile his aide-de-camp, Alfred-Ingemar Berndt (who had been a high official in the Propaganda Ministry and had good contacts with the senior leadership), worked behind the scenes. Hitler relented and gave his consent to the retreat, 'given how the situation has developed, I also approve of your decision.'[64]

Rommel later wrote that he had felt compelled to suspend the retreat because he expected unquestioning obedience from his men and therefore had to give the same. Hitler had resented Rommel's operating on his own authority and had given his approval grudgingly, despite verbally praising the retreat as 'exemplary and fantastic'. He finally realised that the retreat, in which the Axis forces pulled back 1,200 kilometres by the end of November, was a better delaying tactic, tying down enemy forces and giving time for broader strategic decisions.

Rommel must have realised from this episode that not all of the Führer's orders made military sense. Differences with Hitler flared up several more times beginning in the autumn of 1942 because of his orders forbidding any retreat. One

Furious at Hitler's order to hold out. The 'Desert Fox' with Italian officers.

example was when the situation for the German-Italian Panzerarmee became even more precarious when the Allies invaded Morocco and Algeria on 8 November 1942. Rommel took the spontaneous decision to fly to Hitler and suggest abandoning North Africa in a massive evacuation. Without Hitler's prior approval he made his way to Führer Headquarters at Rastenburg together with Berndt at the end of November 1942. In the presence of his General Staff Hitler screamed at his Field Marshal, 'you are suggesting exactly the same thing as the generals did in Russia in 1941/42. I did not do it then and was proven right. I will not do it here either, as I have to take into consideration the political consequences.'[65] Rommel hit back and pointed out in the strongest language possible that the army's total loss would be unavoidable if it remained in North Africa. One cannot fight against tanks with rifles, he told Hitler, and challenged him to come to see for himself. This was too much for Hitler. He threw Rommel out of the situation conference. Rommel left the room 'like a drowned poodle' wrote the Führer's orderly Heinz Linge.[66] However, Hitler personally ran after the Desert Fox and mumbled a few apologetic words like 'All of our nerves are probably a bit on edge', with the result that the meeting continued. Abandoning North Africa was off the table. Instead Hitler promised more reinforcements, which of course never materialised.

After two years of battle in Africa the Field Marshal was physically exhausted. Rommel was increasingly disturbed by the developments in North Africa and the realisation how little 'his Führer', whom he had followed without question, valued his advice. Göring came to the conclusion that Rommel had 'absolutely lost his nerve' after the two had travelled to Rome in Göring's luxurious special train.[67] Hitler had come to the conclusion that 'One cannot leave a man in a very difficult position of responsibility for too long. In time it demoralises his nerves. There is a difference if one is far away behind the lines. . . . That is why I have decided to replace . . . a whole row of generals now, who are actually quite good, and simply order them, even a Field Marshal, to take so many months leave, so that they will come back completely recovered.'[68]

At home in Wiener Neustadt. With his son Manfred and wife Lucie.

Rommel, whom Hitler said had become 'the greatest pessimist',[69] was actually so depressed that he could hardly carry on when he returned to the North African front. He watched the continually deteriorating situation almost lethargically. In mid-January he finally sent his trusted intermediary Berndt to Führer Headquarters one more time, where Hitler was totally immersed in trying to solve the winter crisis on the Russian Front. Goebbels noted, 'Berndt returns from the Führer Headquarters in the evening and makes his report to me. He has explicitly laid out Rommel's plans to Hitler. Even if all available forces have to go east, the Führer understands that something fundamental has to be done for North Africa . . . Unfortunately a whole row of differences has developed between Marshal Rommel and Marshal Kesselring . . . Most of all, Kesselring could not fulfil his promise at the 11th hour. As a result Rommel finds himself in a very embarrassing situation, as he has final responsibility for the ground battle and Kesselring is taking the easy way out, feigning optimism, because he does not have to make the final decision. Berndt takes the opportunity of report to present to the Führer all these things, and the Führer has great sympathy for Berndt's explanation. He assures Rommel once again of his 100 per cent confidence.'[70]

Berndt hurriedly returned to North Africa to report this to Rommel, and Hitler enhances his status by appointing Rommel Commander-in-Chief of Army Group Africa at the end of February, but this did little to alter Rommel's state of mind. Berndt showed his concern in a letter to Rommel's wife when he wrote, 'the Marshal's situation is causing depression, in which he sees everything differently than it is, darker, more unfavourably.' In an effort to sound encouraging he adds that he would like to 'reassure him that he is well thought of in all quarters.'[71]

Rommel found himself in a quandary. On the one hand, there was the faint hope of possibly saving the army, on the other the foreboding that if he did not get a free hand to manoeuvre, more than 70,000 German soldiers would march into captivity. Once again he tried to explain his position in a detailed radio message to Hitler. He wanted, at the very least, to reduce the front line drastically and concentrate his defence at a bridgehead in Tunis. But Führer Headquarters dismissed the request. Hitler, backed by his Wehrmacht Chief of Staff, Jodl, who called the plan 'preposterous', summarily rejected his Field Marshal's pleas. Rommel decided it was time to take the 'cure holiday' that had been previously decided on. He boarded a plane in Sfax to fly to the Führer Headquarters at Vinnitsa in the Ukraine via Rome, taking Berndt with him. On 8 March 1943 Rommel left Africa forever.

The events surrounding Rommel's return reflected the difficulties in his relationship with Hitler, despite the fact that Hitler appeared visibly satisfied with the situation report the Field Marshal delivered at Führer Headquarters on 10 March. Rommel was 'spontaneously' awarded Diamonds to the Knight's Cross, a decoration which was awarded no more than thirty times. Goebbels, who was present at the meeting, noted in his diary, 'He gives him a report, which the Führer likes very much. Rommel has the way open for himself again. The talks with the Führer have gone exceedingly well.'[72] Buoyed up by Hitler's apparent satisfaction, and armed with empty promises, Rommel was prepared to return to Tunisia to organise the defence there, but instead, he was ordered to take several months' holiday without any mention of a future assignment. Even worse for him, the award of the Diamonds was initially kept secret. The pessimist in Rommel concluded that he had fallen out of favour with the Supreme Commander. This seemed confirmed when Hitler did not reply to a birthday telegram sent on 20 April 1943. With rather too obvious optimism the pessimist wished Hitler 'victory on all fronts'.

Notwithstanding this outward optimism, Rommel very quickly demonstrated his real feelings when he gave a realistic, and to Hitler an infuriating, appraisal of the battles at the Tunisian bridgehead. The continued reversals had reduced the Axis's North African positions to this critical state. Hitler had again given a 'no retreat' order to the front. In the meantime Rommel had sent a written appeal to the OKW, suggesting they at least evacuate the most competent officers and experts by air. The appeal fell on deaf ears. His rival, Field Marshal Kesselring, Commander-in-Chief South, was so optimistic that he convinced the High Command that with the expected reinforcements he could hold Tunis without difficulty. Hitler bet on Kesselring's optimism, and lost.

'Rommel has absolutely lost his nerve.' Göring in conversation with Hitler, 1942.

Rommel did not perceive that he might be back in favour with Hitler until his prediction of November 1942 that North Africa would be lost came true when the Axis troops surrendered in mid-May 1943. Hitler ordered Rommel (of whom Goebbels wrote, the development 'is practically breaking his heart'[73]) back to Führer Headquarters after almost two months of silence. Hitler explained that he should have listened to his evacuation suggestions sooner and smoothed over their differences.

There was also an outward indication that the relationship between the two men was improving when Hitler released the news of the award of the Diamonds to the Knight's Cross. It was also announced that Rommel had been in Germany on convalescent leave since the award. The Führer placed 'great importance' on avoiding any association of the Field Marshal with the surrender in Africa, as he did not want his image damaged. Goebbels was delighted that Hitler still had 'such a high opinion of Rommel'. He felt that he could 'be very happy about the announcement the Führer had dictated for him.'[74] Nevertheless Rommel was still 'a bit sad' that Hitler had not made public the customary letter of congratulations that accompanied the medal.

Rommel's mood improved as his relationship with Hitler grew closer during the following months. He was in Hitler's immediate company at Führer Headquarters for weeks at a time during the summer of 1943. They conversed 'very animatedly' with each other as they had in the past. Rommel found that the 'Führer' was 'obviously delighted' to 'have him there' and gave him 'his full trust'. It appears that Hitler's optimism and repeated reference to Rommel's advice worked its magic on him. 'The extraordinary strength which the Führer exudes, his unflustered confidence, the foresighted assessment of the situation . . . have made it very plain in these days that we are all poor souls in comparison to the Führer,' he wrote to his wife in August 1943, searching in his own personality for reasons for his bumpy relationship with Hitler.[75]

However, in the long run the increasingly hopeless situation at the various fronts made further conflict between the men inevitable. Rommel saw a reality that depressed him; Hitler avoided the prospect of defeat and found refuge in phrases like 'holding out' and 'ultimate victory'. Rommel, straightforward and open, could not fit into Hitler's world of self-delusion anymore. Predictably the relationship cooled. Rommel avoided the obvious conclusion and attributed this distancing to Hitler's lack of trust. He searched himself for reasons, but naturally could not find any. Rommel's obtuseness also prevented him from understanding why Kesselring had become more popular with Hitler by October 1943. At issue was the situation in Italy, where Italy's status as an ally of Germany had come

At the special request of the 'Führer'. Convalescent leave in Wiener Neustadt, April 1943.

under threat by the late summer of 1943. At the end of July Hitler had ordered Rommel to oversee a precautionary German advance to the borders of its fragile ally. The fascist regime collapsed catastrophically at the beginning of September and the 'Axis Partner', led by its General Staff, defected to the Allies, who had landed in southern Italy. Rommel (in the north of Italy) and Kesselring (in the south) took over Supreme Command of 'Operation Axis', the occupation of Italian territory. Kesselring believed he could hold up the Allied advance, at least for the winter of 1943/44, at the so-called 'Gustav Line' south of Rome. Jodl agreed, believing the line 'impregnable', but Rommel disagreed; he favoured defending the 'Albert Line' north of Rome. He foresaw the Allies by-passing the Gustav Line with an amphibious landing farther north. Although Hitler opted for Kesselring's plan, he seemed to favour Rommel personally. He told Rommel in mid-October 1943 that he wanted to give him sole command in Italy and transfer Kesselring to the strategically less important Norwegian command. However Rommel, who had even gone so far as to suggest he be given the title of Supreme Commander Italy, forfeited his chance of command at the last moment. He announced to Hitler that before assuming command he would need to make a detailed inspection of Kesselring's positions and then make an 'unvarnished recommendation'. Hitler immediately gave Kesselring Supreme Command Southwest.

In the end Kesselring's more optimistic view was the reason he prevailed over Rommel. Hitler explained his decision at the end of August 1944, during a meeting with two generals; 'At that time he [Rommel] predicted the imminent collapse of Italy. It has not yet happened. He has been proven totally wrong by events and I have been justified in my decision to leave Field Marshal Kesselring there, whom I recognised as an unbelievable political idealist, as well as a military optimist, and I believe you cannot be a military leader without optimism.'[76]

Rommel believed he was slowly gaining Hitler's trust again when he decided to send the Field Marshal (who had incredibly gained popularity with both friend and foe due to both Goebbel's and British propaganda) to the Western Front in November 1943. During an extensive inspection tour Rommel had to familiarise himself with the entire range of incomplete coastal defences facing Great Britain. After the inspection his staff was supposed to develop proposals for improvement and draw up contingency plans in the event of an Allied landing in Western Europe. The scale of the task reinvigorated Rommel, even if he voiced some doubts at

*With faith in victory
in the West. On an
inspection trip at the
'Atlantic Wall', 1944.*

first. 'One does not rightly know whether the new assignment
is supposed to mean a demotion. It seems to be perceived that
way in some quarters. I am reluctant to believe it. The Führer
spoke completely differently. There are so many envious people.
And yet, the time is so critical that any envy and discord is
really inappropriate.'[77]

Slowly Rommel regained his stride again, finding faith in
Hitler and his speeches of 'ultimate victory'. When Hitler made
his annual speech to 'old fighters' in the Munich Beer Hall
Rommel noted, 'What strength he exudes! With what faith and
confidence his people adore him!'[78] This straightforward man
was unable to understand Hitler's world of delusion, a world
where every means was justified to lead Germany to world
domination, and if not to total catastrophe.

'Fighters for the National Socialist future.' The field marshals swearing the oath of loyalty to Hitler.

In January 1944 Rommel was appointed commander of Army Group B, one of the two army groups in France, under Field Marshal Gerd von Rundstedt, Supreme Commander West. When he assumed command he began a feverish effort to strengthen and expand the Atlantic Wall. From his headquarters at the chateau of La Roche Guyon on the Seine, about 60 kilometres upstream of Paris, he co-ordinated an ambitious building programme and undertook extensive inspection trips. He was full of confidence when he wrote his wife in January 1944 that he 'truly believes we will win the defensive battle in the West, if a bit more time to get ready remains,' whilst he had been 'of good hope' on the subject around Christmas time in 1943.[79]

He was present at a high level military meeting at the Berghof on 19 March 1944 where von Rundstedt read to Hitler a declaration of loyalty from his Field Marshals. Goebbels formulated the declaration, which Rommel had signed, in response to the foundation of the anti-fascist Association of German Officers by prisoners in Russia. The rhetoric peaked in a pledge of 'deepest solidarity and unwavering loyalty' to the Führer and National Socialism. They promised to give everything to ensure that 'every soldier of the Army would become an even more fanatical fighter for the National Socialist future of our nation.'[80] The other commanders present saw Hitler as a shadow of his former self, both physically and as an orator, but Rommel felt the Führer's speech given the next day was of 'wonderful clarity and superior calm.'[81]

Rommel felt that his appointment to the Western Front was ideal since he believed, as Hitler did, that the decisive battle of the war would take place there. His pessimism of the previous year seemed to have disappeared, possibly because he was receiving increasing praise from Hitler. Goebbels noted on 14 April 1944, 'The Führer . . . is very enthusiastic about Rommel's work. Rommel has worked with exemplary effect in the West. He has an old score to settle with the British and Americans, is on fire with anger and hate, and has put all his cunning and intelligence into the perfection of the defensive works there. Rommel is the old fighter again.'[82]

Rommel wrote to his wife, with evident pride and satisfaction, that he was quite glad that he had been able to get so involved again after he had been written off as a sick man in various circles. It was apparently very important to him to point out his personal relationship with Hitler when he wrote, 'But the Führer trusts me and that is enough for me.'[83] This perceived trust made him almost burst with optimism in the last weeks before the Allied invasion, 'We have greatest confidence of success in the West,' 'we are getting stronger day by day, . . . I am anticipating the battle with greatest confidence.'[84] He reported progress on the expansion of the defences of the Atlantic Wall to Hitler by telephone on 16 May and Rommel was happy with the reaction of his Supreme Commander, 'He was in the best mood and did not hold back his praise for our work in the West.'[85]

Rommel took advantage of a spell of bad weather, when he was assured that an Allied landing would not take place, to return to the Reich on 4 June 1944. He had hoped for a meeting with Hitler, to request additional Panzer divisions for the defence of the coast. Schmundt told Rommel that the meeting would possibly take place on the morning of 6 June. When Rommel received a telephone call that fateful morning at his home in Herrlingen, where he had made an intermediate stop, the subject was not about the meeting with Hitler, but the beginning of the invasion of Normandy. The decisive battle of the war had started without him.

Futile Initiatives

Rommel immediately returned to La Roche Guyon. Within a few days he came to the sad conclusion that his plan to repulse the invasion forces right at the coast had failed and the defence of 'Fortress Europe' was in great doubt. He had quickly realised that in order to prevent the collapse of the Reich the war on two fronts would have to be ended. There would have to be a cease-fire on one front. His thoughts centred on a political solution with the western powers, believing due to his wartime experiences with them in Africa that the British were fair opponents. In particular he viewed Field Marshal Montgomery as a possible conduit through whom further contacts with the Western Allies might be formed. Like Hitler,

Musing about peace in the West. Rommel after the successful Allied invasion, June 1944.

Rommel considered Bolshevism a danger to the world. He felt the Soviets could not be allowed to win, which is why he hoped Western Europe might still find a way to unite against them.

Rommel broached the necessity of a cease-fire in the West for the first time on 17 June in Margival when he met with Hitler and von Rundstedt. Jodl later testified before the International Military Tribunal at Nuremberg that, 'Rommel especially laid out the seriousness of the situation in France in a totally unmistakable fashion.' The Western Front could not be held much longer. Rommel closed his analysis of the situation with an urgent demand that the war in the West be brought to an end by political means. Hitler, usually surrounded by sycophantic General Staff officers, was not used to such a forceful presentation, which is why he angrily reproached Rommel: 'That is a question that does not pertain to your duties. You have to leave that to me.'[86] Then Hitler did an about-face and, as his Luftwaffe Adjutant, von Below, reported, exercised 'all his skill to persuade Rommel of the opposite'.[87] Hitler eloquently described all the new wonder weapons now coming into full deployment, the rockets and jet fighters, that would bring about a turning-point in the war and create more favourable conditions for a political settlement. When Rommel left headquarters he was back in his old mood and totally in the thrall of 'his Führer'. The Field Marshal wrote to his wife, 'saw the Führer yesterday . . . I am now looking forward to the future with far less worry than I did a week ago. The V-weapon attack was a great relief. A quick breakthrough to Paris by the enemy is hardly a possibility anymore. We will now receive a lot of reinforcements. The Führer was very nice and in a good mood. He definitely recognises the seriousness of the situation.'[88]

Rommel's staff realised when he returned that he was rein-vigorated. Naval Liaison Officer to Army Group B, Vice-Admiral Friedrich Ruge, who had frequent conversations with Rommel during these days, noted that Hitler was still exerting an 'actual magnetism'. Everything seemed to be in a state of intoxication.[89] But this feeling passed quickly and the sober reality of the crumbling resistance to the invasion once again consumed the Field Marshal. He mused to Ruge, enquiringly as well as in anticipation, that the 'Führer' must 'now soon come to this conclusion. But he evades decisions. Always only ordering "hold to the last man" does not get results since the troops will not co-operate in the long run.'[90]

Rommel made his point that a political resolution was absolutely necessary in even stronger terms than at the Margival conference when he met with Hitler on 29 June at the Berghof. It was their last encounter, and it ended in an argument. Rommel tried three times to voice his opinion on the dramatic development of the situation. When he finally got a chance to speak his piece and outline Germany's relative combat weakness, Hitler reprimanded his Field Marshal. He was only to speak about the military situation, he screamed at Rommel. When Rommel continued his explanations about the necessity for a cease-fire, Hitler finally ordered him to leave the room. Rommel's dejection was apparent to all around him when he returned to La Roche Guyon. Ruge summarised the little information Rommel shared with him about his futile meetings with Hitler, 'Nothing much was mentioned at breakfast . . . The Führer said he had not really believed his reports of English battle tactics in North Africa. Realisation comes a bit late! Führer himself apparently quite calm. Situation was assessed as not being that bad.'[91]

In early July the situation in France became even worse and Rommel felt compelled to write a ten-page analysis on the progress of the invasion to date, which he forwarded to Hitler by way of his contact at Führer Headquarters, Schmundt. As in previous situations, the Field Marshal believed Hitler would take appropriate action. However, he became more and more worried that Hitler might not act, and decided to try another approach. On 15 July he wrote a two-page document for Hitler's attention that described the possibility of the Allies breaking through his thinly-stretched defences and advancing into the 'breadth of French territory' in the foreseeable future. The increasingly depressed Field Marshal ended with the urgent appeal: 'The troops are fighting valiantly everywhere, yet the unequal battle is nearing its end. In my opinion it is necessary to see the implications of this situation. I feel myself obligated to state this clearly, as Supreme Commander of the Army Group.'[92]

Rommel forwarded this second analysis through official channels, which meant through Field Marshal Günther von Kluge, von Rundstedt's successor as Supreme Commander West. Kluge added a covering note to Hitler, dated 21 July 1944, pointing out he had been in command now for only 14 days. He reported he had carried out detailed briefings with responsible commanders, particularly SS commanders of various areas of the front, and reluctantly concluded Rommel was correct. In the face of Allied air superiority he thought the concern for the front in the West was justified. Despite the greatest efforts the moment was coming when the overtaxed front would collapse. As the Supreme Commander responsible, he believed it was his duty to bring this situation to the Führer's attention in time.

Two days after Rommel had sent the report, and three days before Colonel Claus Graf von Stauffenberg's assassination attempt on Hitler, ground-attack aircraft attacked Rommel's vehicle during an inspection trip southeast of Caen near Livarot in Normandy. The fighter-bombers approached from the rear and opened fire at extremely close range. Rommel is said to have looked directly at them with utter disgust. What happened seconds later is summarised in a report as follows: 'The aircrafts' bursts of fire primarily hit the left side of the vehicle with high explosive shells. One high explosive shell shattered the driver's left shoulder. Rommel was injured in the face by glass splinters and was struck on the left temple and the cheekbone, which among other things caused a threefold fracture at the base of the skull and led to immediate loss of consciousness. Due to his serious injury Daniel, the driver, lost control of the car; first he crashed into a tree on the right side

On an inspection tour in southwestern France. In the driver's seat, Daniel, who lost his life during the air attack on Rommel, May 1944.

of the road, then he veered at a sharp angle into the ditch on the left side. Field Marshal Rommel, who had been holding the door handle in his right hand at the beginning of the attack, was hurled unconscious out of the car during this manoeuvre and lay on the right side of the road 20 metres behind the car . . . In order to get immediate medical treatment for the injured, Captain Lang tried to secure a vehicle, but it took him three quarters of an hour. The Field Marshal was treated by a French medic at a hospital run by a religious order in Livarot who diagnosed the Field Marshal's injury as very serious and had grave doubts about his survival.'[93]

When the seriously injured Rommel finally awoke from his coma in the hospital in Bernay he learned of the attempt on Hitler's life at the Wolfsschanze. The soldier Rommel, who had praised loyalty and regarded it as his first principle, found the attempted assassination a disgrace to the primarily aristocratic officers who had taken part. To his long-serving adjutant he said that he could only be grateful to 'Providence' that the Führer was spared for the German nation.[94] He also expressed his consternation in a letter to his wife, 'In addition to my accident, the attempted assassination of the Führer has shaken me particularly hard. One can only thank God that it all went so well. I had forwarded my opinion shortly before.'[95]

On the day before he wrote his wife, Rommel (who had been moved yet again, this time to a hospital in Le Vésinet near Paris) received a visit from von Kluge. There is no way of knowing exactly what the two men discussed, but the Supreme Commander West told his chief of staff, General Günther Blumentritt, 'Rommel expressed his surprise that someone had tried to kill Hitler, which was something completely different from exerting pressure on him so he would ask for peace'.[96]

On the same day Rommel spoke to Ruge, who had written in his diary before he knew whether Hitler had survived, 'that's not how one solves questions of fate'.[97] Rommel announced that he intended to travel to Hitler as soon as he possibly could to press him to permit a meeting with Montgomery. Rommel repeated this intention several times as he slowly recuperated. The wounded Field Marshal, who had constantly remained loyal to Hitler despite their differences of opinion, still had not given up hope of persuading 'his Führer' to make peace in the West. The intended meeting never took place because Hitler, who had just sent his injured Field Marshal a get-well telegram, soon received information suggesting his general was one of the conspirators of 20 July.

2

The Army Commander

When cadets cited Clausewitz's *On War* (the 'bible' of general staff officers) in Rommel's classes during his War College days, he used to reprimand them, 'Do not concern yourselves with what Clausewitz meant. What do you think?'[1] Clausewitz could not really contribute to a better understanding of modern tactical warfare. On the other hand he could contribute insights into the understanding of war, as the Prussian military theorist had stated that war was the continuation of politics by other means. This required the close co-ordination of political and military leadership – in other words strategy – and that great commanders be able to think politically. This had not happened during the First World War. Since the army leadership understood little of politics, and the politicians nothing of warfare, and the co-ordination between them was exceptionally poor, it resulted in the inglorious end of the war for Germany. In the view of many contemporaries this inglorious end was entirely out of proportional to the military situation.

The apolitical training in the Reichswehr had maintained the separation between politics and the military, making it easy for the National Socialists to completely exclude the Army as a political factor and to implement a style of leadership

The pragmatist. *Rommel was less interested in von Clausewitz, the Prussian military theorist.*

whereby even army commanders were told only enough to carry out their orders. They were granted neither access to nor participation in the development of strategy, being relegated to mere instruments. Even the General Staff officers surrounding the Führer were often simply stooges who could be replaced or sent into the 'Führer Reserves' if they dared to challenge him. Political and military leadership were concentrated in one man, whom they consequently tended to call 'the greatest field commander of all times' – Hitler himself.

The Would-Be Strategist

Like most generals, although he spent many months in the Führer Headquarters, Rommel did not know that Hitler's politics and strategy in war had one aim, based on an essentially finalised plan. This plan was to create an empire extending across all of continental Europe with colonial 'territory for expansion'. Rommel did not know that smashing the Soviet Union and major territorial acquisitions in the East would be the cornerstone of this plan. Nor did Rommel realise that Hitler saw no conflict of interest between Germany and the maritime power Great Britain, which he hoped to make an ally. He envisioned joining with it, after the elimination of the Soviet Union, in order to compete with Europe's only remaining challenger for global hegemony: the United States of America.

When the British Prime Minister, Neville Chamberlain, declared war on 3 September 1939, he did it because he saw the cherished British concept of the European balance of power threatened after Germany invaded Poland. Rommel had no idea that Hitler's strategy had already gone awry. The Führer had hoped to the very end that London would 'hold still' and that he would be able to defeat his abhorrent neighbour in the East in a short campaign. However, after both Great Britain and France had declared war, he was stuck with a war on two fronts. Rommel looked only at the situation in Poland, which was crumbling under the onslaught of Germany and its Bolshevik ally, under the terms of the Hitler–Stalin pact. He wrote his wife on 9 September 1939, 'In my opinion I should be home by the time winter arrives. The war is going quite according to plan. The boldest expectations are being surpassed. The Russians will probably attack in the near future. Two million men!'[2]

Despite the overthrow of Poland in a quick campaign, Rommel did not get home by winter. Hitler's war expanded piecemeal across all of Europe. Soon the Reich's flag was flying over Norway and Denmark. In the spring of 1940, the Wehrmacht began an unparalleled run of victories in the West. Again Rommel looked only at the phenomenal military victory over France. He had no idea that Hitler hoped to 'corner' Great Britain through this. Why should it dawn on the General that one conquered France in order to make the British leadership ready for peace? Particularly when Hitler announced his desire to annihilate Great Britain and sent Göring's Luftwaffe into the 'Great Battle' against England in the late summer of 1940?

When Rommel took over command of the Afrika Korps in February 1941 he grossly misunderstood Great Britain's place in Hitler's overall strategy. Rommel's assignment in North Africa was to 'bring the advance of the enemy units to a halt and defeat them with the offensive deployment of tank forces.'[3] 'Enemy units' meant the British, who had gone on the offensive after Rome had declared war on London and begun an attack against Egypt. In fact the British had advanced to within a few hundred kilometres of Tripoli and it seemed they were unstoppable.

Before the dangerous crossing. German troop transports in Naples harbour.

By sending German troops to prevent the loss of all North Africa, Hitler hoped to bolster his 'axis' with the Italians and gain time for the defeat of the Soviet Union, through which he expected in turn to be able to isolate Great Britain. To put it differently, with the annihilation of the Soviet Union, Hitler wanted to show Winston Churchill that it would be pointless for his country and Empire to continue in their war with Germany. The German dictator now exploited his primary target in the east in order to achieve what had been the original prerequisite for his attempt: the settlement with Great Britain.

Once again, in the spring of 1941 Rommel was totally ignorant of the impending Russian campaign. In fact, he thought he was posted to a key position, to the last remaining ground theatre of the war against the only one of the Reich's enemies still left, Great Britain. Based on this misjudgement, and eager to show his mettle, he interpreted Hitler's orders as a command to defeat the Empire's troops as quickly as possible and take Egypt and the Suez Canal. Honestly believing that he would receive sufficient reinforcements, particularly more divisions, he pressed on to the east immediately. He took this course of action despite the fact Hitler had clearly explained to him in a meeting at Führer Headquarters on 21 March that there should be no large-scale operations and that no further reinforcements would be sent to North Africa until the autumn of 1941. However, during this meeting Hitler did not mention anything about the impending Russian campaign. 'Since 31 March,' Rommel wrote to his wife, 'we have attacked with remarkable success. The staffs in Tripoli, Rome and perhaps Berlin will be amazed. I dared, against earlier orders and directions, to go forward because I saw an opportunity. They will approve of it in the end.'[4]

By mid-April Tobruk had been surrounded by the numerically weak German troops, and another element was advancing on the Egyptian border. But the manpower of the corps that had been sent to Africa for defensive purposes was not sufficient for Rommel's offensive. Unit after unit used itself up in his command in repeated attacks on the fortress at Tobruk. For the first time during the Second World War a German army was in danger of being wiped out completely. At the end of April the Army Chief of Staff Halder sent his Quartermaster General, Friedrich von Paulus, who would later surrender at Stalingrad, to North Africa 'in order to bring the soldier who had gone insane back to reason'.[5] Both Halder and von Paulus were only too willing to blame Rommel, whom they did not think up to the job, for the difficulties that had developed.

Rommel's first 'Command Vehicle'. He reconnoitred Tripolitania in this BMW.

They proposed, in vain of course, that he be dismissed. Rommel, who was zealously intent on trying to demonstrate his capabilities in war, defied them because he was operating under false premises, ignorant of overall strategy.

This lack of understanding continued, when Hitler had to 'insert' another attack, a few hundred kilometres farther north in the Balkans, prior to his assault on the Soviet Union. Rommel believed he had found the reason why he had not received the required reinforcements. He wrote to his wife on 22 April 1941 that he believed the Balkan campaign, like his own mission, was designed to reduce the British Suez positions. 'Greece will be taken care of shortly. And then it will be possible to give me more help here. The battle for Egypt is only just beginning.'[6] It quickly became apparent that Rommel continued to fumble in the dark. What actually started, weeks later, was the invasion of Russia. Although the mood of his staff was beginning to turn pessimistic about the outcome of the war, Rommel appeared optimistic. He confidently counted on Hitler for a quick victory. 'A blow against Russia, which did not suit Churchill,' he wrote, and suggested to his wife, 'I probably should not show up at Führer Headquarters with my worries.'[7] As the reinforcements for North Africa continued to fail to materialise, Rommel had to delay his plan to conquer Egypt. Only when the campaign against Soviet Russia turned into a war of attrition in the winter of 1941/42 did Rommel finally realise that he was conducting a sideshow, the fate of which was unalterably dependent of the outcome of the Russian war.

It was more with wishful thinking than realistic consideration that he saw in North Africa the key to a solution of the 'Russian problem'. He developed a war plan, which he described in his 1944 review of the North Africa campaign. According to this plan, after securing air superiority in the Mediterranean, units from France, Norway and Denmark, supplemented by a 'few' Panzer and motorised divisions should be transferred to his command. Thanks to this he envisioned that the following would have occurred: 'We could have beaten and annihilated the British ground forces. With this the path to the Suez Canal would have been clear. . . . After occupation of the entire Mediterranean coast the transport of reinforcements to North Africa could have succeeded practically uninterrupted. Then it would have been possible to advance into Persian and Iraqi territory with the objective of cutting the Russians off from Basra, taking possession of the oil fields and creating a staging point against the Russian Empire for ourselves. . . . As a final strategic goal one would have had initiated an attack on the

Died for 'Führer, Nation and Fatherland'. Funeral service in the desert.

southern front of the Caucasus in order to take Baku, including the oil fields. That way one would have crippled the Russians. . . . This would have provided the strategic prerequisites to smash the Russian colossus with concentric blows.'[8] Rommel's concept, which of course was based on insufficient information, was naturally rejected by Hitler. Such a 'fantasy', which is how the OKW labelled Rommel's plan, clearly showed how limited his geographical perspective was, and also demonstrated his limited view of the total theatre of war. Presumably the British and the Americans were united in their desire to protect the Middle East with its oil reserves, whatever it might cost. Additionally, Rommel's proposal required dividing German war resources that were already extremely insufficient for the Russian campaign. Even if the resources had been available, the undertaking would have been ruled out due to Hitler's racially-motivated fixation on the destruction of the Soviet

Union. Moreover it implied the destruction of the British global empire, which Hitler did not want. He continued to hope for a settlement with Great Britain and consequently approved no more than limited advances in North Africa that might force London to yield.

Rommel's successes in North Africa fell in with Hitler's overall strategy only when his un-reinforced troops forced the British into dire straits. Rommel's April Offensive in 1941 and the accompanying pressure on London permitted Hitler to hope that Britain might yield. In January and early February 1942 the German General drove the British, who had been weakened in the Mediterranean by Japan's entry into the war, out of Cyrenaica. At that point Hitler was convinced that Churchill would fall, primarily because of the setbacks in the Far East. He believed the subsequent government, perhaps pro-German, would soon end the war with the Reich. In this Hitler was indulging in a fair amount of wishful thinking; his campaign against the Soviet Union had just run afoul of the Russian winter. His hoped-for settlement with Great Britain became vital if he were to win the war in the East on the second attempt.

On 5 February 1942, Hitler told General Walther Nehring, who was in transit from the Russian Front on his way to a new command in North Africa, that it was critical to take Tobruk and advance as far as possible. He believed that threatening Egypt, given the background of British setbacks in the Far East, would increase British interest in peace. At that point another obstacle got in the way of a further advance by Rommel. Mussolini, the nominal supreme commander of the North African theatre of war, had no inclination to spend more of his manpower and materiel assets, and wanted to wait

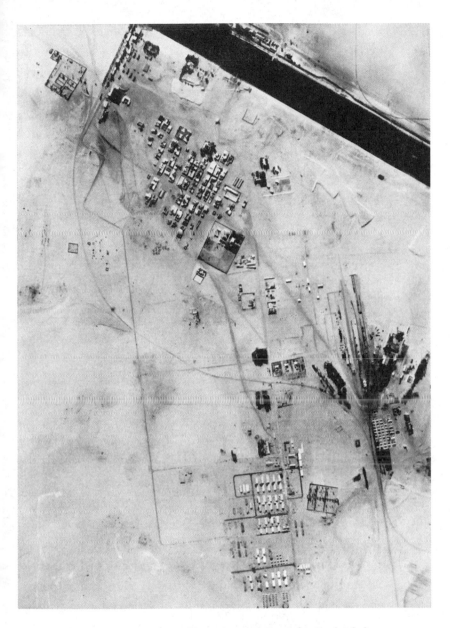

Aerial photography by a German reconnaissance plane, showing bomb damage to a British base at the Suez Canal.

for the expected German victory over the Soviet Union. He declared in no uncertain terms that he expected Germany to follow the guidelines he had issued; the primary mission of the Italian-German troops was to be the defence of Tripolitania. Hitler finally had to forbid his General any further advances because of the need to maintain the relationship with his ally, which was in danger due to Rommel's stubbornness. Hitler could not afford to lose Italy as part of the Axis, which could have disastrous and far-reaching consequences on the southern periphery of Europe, given the catastrophic situation of the German armies in the East.

For a third time North Africa had to fit into the strategic calculations of Hitler, who was totally focused on a 'second attempt in the East.' Rommel finally took Tobruk in June 1942. Hitler spoke of 'destiny's help for the German nation',[9] and von Ribbentrop's State Secretary, Ernst von Weizsäcker, parroted him. He wrote, 'The sudden surrender of Tobruk and the further developments during Rommel's advance pose the question, whether a collapse has started among the English. Will Britain's social framework and the alliance structure of such heterogeneous parties reach disintegration? That would truly open important perspectives. I believe that, in about the next year, beginning in Europe, the nonsense of this war could stop.'[10] But all the hopes tied up in Rommel's advance went up in smoke when the German-Italian advance was stopped at El Alamein.

The strategic evaluations of Hitler and Rommel coincided for a fourth and last time in the spring of 1944, when the concern was the defence of France against an Allied invasion. Personally, the Field Marshal wanted to exact revenge on the British for the defeat in North Africa. Strategically, both he and Hitler

92

Overestimated in its importance: the fall of Tobruk. Captured British troops after the surrender, June 1942.

expected that a victory in the West would allow Germany to concentrate all its forces in the East to withstand the onslaught of the Red Armies. Dwight D. Eisenhower, the Supreme Commander of the Allied Expeditionary Forces, wrote about the consequences of the failure of an invasion in his memoirs. 'Such a catastrophe could have required the complete redeployment of the American armed forces assembled in Great Britain and their transfer to other theatres of war, while the morale and determination of Allied troops would have suffered to an incalculable extent. In the end such a failure would have had an extremely strong impact on the situation in Russia and the thought could not be dismissed that this country would have considered a separate peace . . .'[11]

However, just a few days after the Allied landings in Normandy, it became clear that the Anglo-American armies would be unstoppable. At that point Rommel believed he could lead Hitler to rational behaviour, i.e. ending hostilities in the West, but he was totally ignorant of two factors. First, he was unaware of the requirement by the anti-Hitler coalition for an unconditional surrender by Germany. Second, he did not comprehend that the actual motivating force for the war was Hitler's preoccupation with the racial global conspiracy. The former First World War corporal believed the war had been a struggle of races for existence or annihilation from the very beginning. In his maniac world of illusion the alternative to 'ultimate victory' was an unavoidable 'doom', and not just Germany's. Previously Hitler had written in his *Mein Kampf*, 'Should the Jew, with the aid of his Marxist creed, triumph over the people of this world, his crown will be the funeral dance of mankind, and this planet will once again follow through its orbit through the ether, without any human life on its surface, as it once did millions of years ago.'[12]

The Operational Leader

As little as the Führer allowed his commanders in the field the latitude to be strategists, still less did he condone their exhibiting independent leadership in operations. The plans of operations were developed in the Führer Headquarters and sent to the generals for their execution. Hitler even got involved in the details. This even applied to the Western campaign and the defensive battle in Normandy. The only exception was created by the situation in North Africa, where the German commander was formally subordinate to the Italian Supreme Command but where Germany gained increasing control after the military setbacks suffered by the

Italian fascists. In the confusion over areas of responsibility Rommel was able to create scope for action that no other German commander was able to attain in a Second World War theatre of operations, enabling him to distinguish himself as a bold operational leader. Mobile war leadership, operational leadership, had to dominate. The prerequisites for systematic overall higher-level leadership, such as the British used, were absent for the Axis in North Africa because of its chronic supply shortages.

Rommel quickly realised that the barren, expansive deserts of North Africa provided an ideal terrain for his methods, in contrast to those of the General Staff, which had been valid until then. Away from the focus on the Russian theatre of war, he was able to use his tanks for months on end to compensate for his materiel inferiority, and frequently put his opponent in extreme difficulty. This was so, Rommel explained in 1944, because, 'every success, which is not achieved just through material superiority, has its origin not only in the planning of the winning command, setting aside the courage of the troops, but also in the acts which are not the contribution of the victor, but can properly be labelled the mistakes of the vanquished.'[13] This applied to North Africa, where the mechanical leadership style of the British enabled German victories. A British general who fought against Rommel confirmed this, 'The Germans were far superior to their opponent in their ability to make rapid decisions and move quickly . . . The British generals were not less capable than the Germans. But their military training was outdated. It was training grounded in the static positional warfare of the 1914–1918 campaign and not on the mobile war with tanks which they now had to lead.'[14]

Operationally far superior. German Panzers in Cyrenaica.

Rommel's operational success was based primarily on concentrating his forces, supplemented by flexible battle leadership. He showed this in his advance in April 1941 which brought him to the gates of Tobruk and beyond, to the Egyptian border. He repeatedly demonstrated his superior operational leadership during the British offensive of the same year. Although the British were able to surprise Rommel tactically, they did not show any skill in exploiting their advantage. The tank units were separated in a fanlike formation, and this did not provide sufficient concentration at any point to break through Rommel's defensive lines. The British also failed to surround and annihilate Rommel during his weeks-long retreat because they did not advance quickly enough, even though they were well supported logistically. The German General, on the other hand, was able to inflict heavy losses on his opponents, with quick counterattacks by concentrated tank units. He could slow down the British resupply, and gain time for an orderly retreat, particularly for the non-motorised Italian troops. These tactics exhausted the British on their advance, which covered more than 1,000 kilometres. Rommel, for his part, was able to gather his strength for a counter-offensive, which he initiated in January 1942. This move surprised both friend and foe, and he was to retake the huge territorial gains of the British by mid-February.

The Germans' mobile tactics stood in contrast to the more systematic approach of the British army, but it had one serious disadvantage: they could not ensure that the supply train would be able to keep up with the troops. This was particularly evident in Rommel's daring operations. Previously even in the Western campaign it had proven difficult to provide petrol for the rapidly advancing Panzer units. This problem threatened

*Field marshals
amongst themselves.
Rommel and
Kesselring, whose air
force was supposed to
secure the supply lines.*

disaster in North Africa, where supply lines included long sea
crossings and extensive land travel. Back in Rommel's obsti-
nate Spring Offensive in 1941, with its strength being drained
by the battle for Tobruk, the logistics chain literally collapsed.
'Supply situation extremely grave. Troops less than full complement of ammunition. Stocks in Cyrenaica not worth mentioning, in Tripoli too far away . . . Bridging of path to Tripoli
Front with columns of the Afrika Korps totally out of the
question,' reads one Afrika Korps signal.[15]

The supply situation, and consequently Rommel's relationship with those responsible, grew continuously more strained
during the summer of 1941 when the only German air corps in
the region was transferred from southern Italy to the East. The
result was total British control of the central Mediterranean
from their base on Malta; a control so complete that Axis
convoys literally became suicide missions, if they put to sea at
all. The sea transport situation in the Mediterranean only eased

at the end of 1941 when the British diverted some of their forces to the Far East after the Japanese declaration of war and when a Luftwaffe unit (desperately needed in Russia) returned to Kesselring's command on New Year's Eve 1941/42. But the problems of the previous year continued, despite the sea lanes being more open. Rommel's partially refreshed units advanced so fast that the meagre supplies available could not keep up with them. On 6 February 1942, both of Rommel's motorised brigades were immobilised, fuel tanks empty, before the British rearguard at the eastern edge of Cyrenaica, short of supplies and totally exhausted.

As in the previous year, Rommel had provoked conflict with the Italian Supreme Command due to his impetuous, logistically-unsound offensive. It would not allow its own divisions to close up with Rommel instead pushing for an invasion of Malta, which Kesselring's bombers had been systematically attacking. After a four-week long 'great battle' against the air and sea base, the Axis allies agreed to start the offensive against Tobruk in June 1942, and after that to capture Malta in order to establish the logistical stability needed for the later conquest of Egypt. Mussolini and Hitler confirmed the outcome of these negotiations when they met at the end April in Klessheim, but Hitler did not for a second seriously consider risking the invasion of Malta. The extremely heavy losses he had incurred during the conquest of Crete persuaded him to avoid any such further operations. Whilst he pretended to approve of 'Operation Hercules', the codename given to the capture of Malta, he did so to pave the way for his General's immediate attack on Tobruk, an attack the Italian Supreme Command would otherwise have refused to support.

When Rommel, after a month of rest and recuperation, renewed the offensive against Tobruk, he used the same plan he had developed the prior year. While the Italian forces feigned an attack from the west, he sent his fast-moving units off on a wide-ranging encircling manoeuvre. After Bir Hacheim, the defensive outpost south of Tobruk, fell, the Panzerarmee broke into the defences from there, heading north. Tobruk surrendered after a short battle on 20 June 1942. According to the agreement Operation Hercules should have been launched immediately; a plan of operations had already been drawn up. But the recently promoted Field Marshal now urged a continuation of the offensive. He argued that the enemy was already beaten and that the renewed threat from Malta to his supply lines could be ignored because he could use the supplies and materiel captured at Tobruk. He foresaw being able to make a surprise advance, which could culminate in a few days with the conquest of lower Egypt.

The emphasis on manoeuvre over logistics reached its fatal peak in the aftermath of victory in the battle for Tobruk. Doubts that supplies could be brought forward fast enough were disregarded. The illusion prevailed that sufficient quantities, particularly of fuel, could be delivered through convoys on the eastern routes to Benghazi, supplemented by increased use of transport submarines and aircraft. Rommel obtained Hitler's agreement, and he in turn that of Mussolini, over the protests of the Italian Supreme Command and Kesselring.

When Rommel crossed the Egyptian border in pursuit of the retreating enemy he was in short supply of everything – fuel, transport capacity and tanks, as well as lacking air support. The result was that as early as 24 June, when the spearhead of the Panzerarmee, which had only about sixty operational combat

100

Far from home. Soldiers of the Afrika Korps in front of a first aid post.

vehicles, reached Sidi-Barani, the Royal Air Force was able to attack it unopposed. It suffered heavy losses in men and materiel. On the following day the units had to pause motionless for hours in the Egyptian desert for lack of fuel. Rommel, who did not have the benefit of radio reports due to the rapid retreat of the British Eighth Army, and ignoring Kesselring's warnings, was convinced he could reach Cairo by the end of the month. Initially it looked as though he were right as the advance continued; on 27 June 1942 his units rolled into Marsa Matru. Three days later the army formed up for an attack on El Alamein. Alexandria was only 150 kilometres beyond.

Rommel's adversary, Montgomery, knew why he had to make his primary line of defence at El Alamein. It was only there that his opponent would not be able to count on his operational superiority. The sea on one flank and the steep drop-off of the Qattara Depression on the other made German outflanking manoeuvres impossible. Rommel was forced to make a frontal attack, and the first battle of El Alamein became a battle of attrition. The attacker was not up to it. After two days and nights of battle Rommel was forced to report to the OKW that 'the strength of the enemy, minimal own fighting strength and very strained supply situation' would force the Panzerarmee to abandon the attack. Rommel's 'dream of the Nile' was finally put to an end.[16]

El Alamein marked the turning-point in the African campaign; when the British moved to the offensive in November 1942 Rommel finally had to give ground. Yet even during the long retreat to Tunisia he was able to severely hit the methodically advancing Empire troops repeatedly due to his superior operational leadership. Even though the Africa campaign was finally lost, this was originally not due as much to the difficulties of delivering supplies as the lack of supplies themselves, although in the later stages even the transport resources dwindled.

In 1944 Allied air dominance in the West in particular caused Rommel to want to move away from the concept of mobile battle leadership for the defence of the coastal section stretching from north of the Loire to the Netherlands, which was under his command as Commander of Army Group B. This countered the operational expectations of the Supreme Commander West, von Rundstedt. The German troops stationed in France were insufficient to both completely protect the coast and at the same time maintain an adequate operational reserve in the interior. Thus, von Rundstedt, in accordance with a plan developed by the OKW, intended to keep the available Panzer and motorised divisions in the interior of France so they could be moved quickly to the site of the Allied landings.

Fear of Allied air superiority. Rommel watches enemy bombers, June 1944.

The plan would have been the correct one for Rommel 'under normal conditions' despite the weak coastal defences, and would in all likelihood been successful. But in Rommel's opinion von Rundstedt underestimated the strength of Allied air power, which would prevent the rapid advance of the German units positioned in the interior. 'At El Alamein,' Rommel wrote, 'we had sufficient opportunity to be able to study the impact of the Anglo-American bomber tactics on our motorised units. In France it is to be expected that the air power deployed on invasion day will be far greater than the bomber squadrons that were available to the Allies in North Africa. In contrast to the African desert terrain only a few roads in France, which lead over rivers and through towns, could be used for the advance. That is why the effectiveness of the Allied air forces would be significantly greater here than in the desert.'[17]

Keeping air power in mind, Rommel wanted to position the Panzer divisions directly on the coast. That way they could attack the opponent at the weakest moment of the invasion, the time when the troops neared the coast in boats and ships. These locally-deployed forces were designed to prevent the invaders from establishing a beachhead, which would be critical to their resupply. In the meantime, Panzer and motorised units from other sectors could be brought up and assembled behind the threatened front to sweep away the enemy landing sites in a counter-stroke. Rommel was convinced, as he wrote Hitler in March 1944, 'the outcome of the battle will be determined at the coast.'[18] Rommel's predictions met with resistance from the Supreme Commander West and other generals. After months of wrangling a compromise was finally reached. Hitler ordered that only a portion of the Panzer divisions be put under

Rommel's command and moved forward towards the coast. The remaining part was to be held in reserve in the interior under the command of the OKW.

The reason Hitler and the OKW refused to put all the Panzer divisions under Rommel's command was because there was a difference of opinion about where the invasion would take place. Rommel and von Rundstedt were convinced that the Allies would gather for the storming of Fortress Europe at the Pas de Calais, in other words at the narrowest point of the English Channel. In contrast, Hitler had repeatedly pointed to the Normandy coast as the place to expect the landing. Even after the landings had taken place in Normandy, Rommel and von Rundstedt both remained convinced for a long period that this was just a feint to distract from the actual landing, which would take place at the Pas de Calais. General Heinz Guderian, who commanded one of the two Panzer corps in France, remembered, 'we sat there fairly protected. Still north of the Seine, in reserve, were then . . . pushed further toward the Channel coast by Rommel, but not all the way into the invasion front, but to the Channel coast because he [Rommel] always said, "The actual landing is still to come. And it will come here at the Channel coast."' What Guderian did not say was that after 6 June he too still expected the main landing to come at the Pas de Calais. When the Germans finally came to the conclusion that the Channel landing was not going to happen, clear weather and the resultant Allied air dominance prevented the rapid advance of the Panzers to the Normandy front. The invasion forces were thereby able to establish their beachhead, through which a massive, unhindered resupply flowed.

Rommel misjudged the point of the landing and thereby reduced the already slim chances of the defenders of the continent.

He was aware of this and tried to conceal it since he believed he would be held responsible. In the last chapter of his book, *War Without Hate*, which was drafted shortly before his death, he tried to stand truth on its head. He wrote, 'neither the Führer Headquarters nor the Supreme Commander West [wanted] to acknowledge the threat against Normandy, as both assumed that the better strategic opportunities to establish a beachhead at the Pas de Calais would lead the Allies to land there. But the execution of the Anglo-American concept depended on achieving the initial landing, and this probability did not exist in the strongly built-up Pas de Calais, but was practically guaranteed in the barely-fortified Normandy.'[19]

The Tactician

In his operational calculations Rommel always bore in mind the material inferiority of the Wehrmacht. 'There is no art in being a field commander in a rich land which possesses much war material. I, however, have to restrain myself and try to beat my enemy with limited means,' he wrote in April 1944.[20] In Rommel's opinion it was vital to polish his tactics. These he mastered like a virtuoso. He had gained a good basis for this with his analysis of the engagements he had experienced in the First World War. He had developed his lectures based on this analysis while at the Dresden and Potsdam infantry schools and turned them into a noteworthy work on tactics.

Kurt Hesse, a colleague of his at the Dresden Infantry School, later wrote that Rommel should be understood from the perspective of the storming of the Monte Matajur. 'Basically he always remained the same lieutenant in being able to grasp the immediate situation and the lightning fast

106

reaction that came from it.'[21] The underlying thought apparently was surprising the enemy with respect to time and place. In its execution it often meant a daredevil dash forward, as he showed for the first time in the Second World War when he was the newly-appointed commander of the 7th Panzer Division during the French campaign in 1940.

However, Rommel was not satisfied to rest on his laurels. He brooded over how the use of surprise, or feint, could be perfected. In France in 1940 he attacked backlit by the early morning sun. As a result his blinded opponent could not distinguish between friend and foe until it was too late. Rommel's nightly sorties confused the French as much as his breakthrough at the forest of Cerfontaine when his troops adopted the ruse of waving large white flags. At the Meuse he had houses set on fire so he could lead his unit across the river under the cover of the smoke.

Rommel was more inventive than any other general in the Second World War when it came to making more from less, or at least giving that impression. Even today old 'Afrikaner', as the soldiers of the Afrika Korps are called, tell how Rommel tried to make fools of the British with superior tactics. In the very beginning, at the parade of the first units of the Afrika Korps to arrive in Tripoli, he ordered tanks that had already passed in review to form up again at the rear of the parade column to give the impression of a larger fighting force. However, that trick only fooled the Italian and Arab onlookers, since the British had no inkling of the presence of German troops in Africa in February 1941.

Rommel's dummy tanks, which his soldiers in Tripoli fabricated and mounted on Volkswagen chassis, were more effective. Rommel later wrote about it to the Quartermaster General of the General Staff of the Army, von Paulus, telling him that though he was short of tanks, the first thirty-five dummies had arrived near the front and would surely confuse the enemy about his actual strength. A further 170 followed the next day. Intercepted enemy message traffic showed that the enemy was actually deceived about the Afrika Korps' strength. To create the impression of operational units where there were none, he had trucks drag tarpaulins through the desert sand behind them to raise large clouds of dust. For the same purpose he installed propellers on vehicles. Around Tobruk he manned observation towers with straw dummies until the British stopped shooting at them. Only then did he allow soldiers to climb the towers.

Rommel demonstrated military technical inventiveness when he created a special defence system for the Atlantic coast. Obstacles shot up of the ground everywhere along the foreshore, including piles with 'can openers' (i.e. iron spurs) fastened on them, wooden stakes with Teller mines as well as concrete and steel tetrahedrons attached to them. He made preparations for enemy airborne landings in the interior. He proudly reported to Hitler in May 1944, 'One corps alone has planted 900,000 posts against enemy airborne landings and has made ready one million grenades to arm the airborne landing obstacles over the next weeks'.[22] These obstacles were known as 'Rommel's asparagus'.

The Superior

To get the most out of unexpected tactical opportunities, Rommel always led from the front. During engagements he travelled back and forth between individual command posts. Five drivers are supposed to have killed in his vehicle beside

Improvised foreshore obstacles against an oppressive superiority. At the French coast.

him. Even when there was heavy enemy air activity he flew over the front in North Africa in his Fieseler Storch, a single-engined scout plane. He once said of himself that he did not lead like a General Staff officer, from a bureaucratic ivory tower. 'The time of a Scydlitz and Zieten has returned. We have to see war from a cavalry perspective – lead tank units like squadrons. Give commands from a moving tank as one used to from the saddle.'[23]

His leadership style, which – according to Rommel – ignored the 'superfluous theoretical stuff'[24] not only presented a danger to his life, but also contained the risk that the co-ordination of the total operation would suffer. It was not unusual for Rommel to be away at the front and not in his command post when he was needed there to make decisions. Yet several military historians certify that he had an 'amazing gift' to suddenly appear at the right place at the right time and give the battle a decisive turn. However, there were other assessments of his conduct, like that of a company commander of a Panzer regiment, who wrote, 'When we saw and heard that Rommel, on days of important battles, preferred to be way up front directing individual tanks and raiding parties instead of with his staff making decisions that the overall situation required . . ., then we asked ourselves whether he really was such a great army leader.'[25]

In his leadership style Rommel remained the dashing soldier of the First World War, even when he became a Field Marshal. From his first command he wanted to be an example to his men and 'take them along'. The young company commander set the example for his men at the battle of Longarone in November 1917 when he was the first to cross the raging and ice-cold Piave River, or later at the storming of Monte Matajur when he fought right at the head of his troops. Rommel was convinced that only by leading from the front could troops be welded together into a unit and imbued with full strength and a good fighting spirit. Each soldier, including himself, had to be willing to take responsibility for the other.

Rommel further developed the combination of capabilities necessary for a leader to achieve his ideal during the 1920s and early 1930s as a company commander and infantry instructor. His assessments in 1928 demonstrate this. 'As instructor and developer of his company he has very good successes to show,' one of his instructors wrote and recommended Rommel as 'instructor for weapons schools'. The ensuing years as tactical instructor at the Dresden Infantry School allowed the previously quiet and humble man to mature into an 'inexhaustively stimulating' and 'infectious leadership type', as the final assessment of the course director noted in 1933.[26]

Part of the reason for his success in this area was due to his pedagogic talent in lecture preparation. Whether consciously or not, he used a presentation technique quite advanced for his time. He placed great emphasis on a varied presentation, in contrast to many of his fellow instructors who often bored the cadets they were instructing. He interspersed his lectures with sketches he had prepared himself projected on to a screen. The schematic presentation of battle situations helped loosen up the class and increase understanding. By using this method, which was unconventional for the time, as well as inspiring his students with tales from the First World War, he struck a nerve in his pupils. In a very short time he became one of the most popular training officers at the Dresden and Potsdam War Colleges. He had the effect of being 'particularly character-building with the objective of developing independence, fresh daring and willingness to take responsibility'. 'A particularly strong influence on youth' was ascribed to him. For many of his cadets his instruction remained 'forever unforgotten', as Nicolaus von Below, Hitler's Luftwaffe Adjutant from 1937 to 1945, wrote in the introduction to his memoirs.[27]

The adulation his students gave Rommel for his actions in the First World War magnified them, while it also concealed the underlying risks. Throughout this period the ever-ambitious Rommel developed an unshakeable self-confidence in his qualifications as a leader of men. As a result of his successes in France and North Africa, and the subsequent promotions by Hitler, the basic philosophy of his military behaviour gradually moved from the militarily achievable to the limits of the possible.

Particularly in Africa Rommel frequently came into conflict with his generals and officers. They were appalled, for example, when he repeatedly ordered attacks on Tobruk in April 1941, in the face of the first futile attempt on the fortress. This had shown the hopelessness of trying to capture it with the weak units he

111

had available. The previously-cited company commander wrote, 'We were inflamed with burning hatred for Rommel when he made us pay for his blind judgement again and again due to his inflexible stubbornness. He sacrificed thousands of lives and irreplaceable materiel in boundless brutality to his personal ambition for no good reason or need. He took us into situations that often threatened the survival of the entire Afrika Korps. He used his authority in an unfair, shameful manner when he demoted responsible men who dared to raise their voices . . . often only to give well intentioned warnings and advice.'[28]

Rommel had Colonel Walter Neumann-Silkow, the commander of one of the Panzer regiments, court-martialled because the officer had suffered a nervous breakdown and refused to attack a far superior English tank unit. He insulted General Kirchheim, who had been decorated with the Pour-le-Mérite, and threatened to have him relieved. He had General Johannes Streich, the commander of the 5th Light Division, relieved, because Rommel believed he was too concerned about protecting the lives of his men. Streich is said to have retorted, 'Actually, greater praise could not be given to a divisional commander.'[29] Complaints about Rommel piled up at OKH. While Halder raged and questioned Rommel's personal qualities, von Brauchitsch felt compelled to reprimand the commander of the Afrika Korps. He sent a radio message saying, 'I have . . . as the result of being presented court martial decisions and complaints, and especially through the numerous requests to relieve officers of high assessment and proven reliability, even taking into consideration the special conditions there and required toughness in leadership in these cases, developed the impression that these measures have not been properly handled. The more difficult the conditions are, the more nerves are stretched. It is all the more the duty of every superior to check closely whether interventions such as threats or requests to relieve battle-proven officers or harsh criticism or hasty orders are appropriate; whether an instructive conversation carried on in a fraternal spirit without any edge to it would be more likely to accomplish the aim. I consider it my duty not only in the interests of the Afrika Korps but also in your personal interest to bring these points to your attention.'[30] Rommel reacted angrily to the reprimand. He would not stand for it, a letter to von Brauchitsch was already on the way, he wrote to his wife, confident of Hitler's support.

Rommel's relationship with his Italian allies was also problematic. Goebbels once noted after a conversation with the Field Marshal, 'Rommel gives the most denigrating judgement of the Italians. He thinks nothing of them.'[31] If this report is correct, his view was based on his experiences with his confederates during the African campaign, and also his experiences in the First World War , when he faced the Italians as enemies at the Isonzo Front. In his tactical manual *Infantry Attacks* he had analysed the Italian defeats. Naturally Rommel attributed them primarily to his superior tactics of attack and surprise, and only secondarily to the failure of Italian commanders. He explained this failure on the basis of National Socialist teachings. 'The War Council of the Masses' undermined the authority of the Italian leaders, wrote Rommel, and drew a narrow parallel to 1918, when German soldiers' councils 'stabbed' the field commanders 'in the back'. Additionally the author specifically pointed out that from the Italian viewpoint 'the war with us Germans was not particularly popular'. Finally he said, 'Today the Italian army is one of the best in the world. It is imbued with a new spirit and has proven its great ability in the

'He has no respect at all for the Italians.' Medal from the ally, spring 1941.

extraordinarily difficult campaign against Abyssinia.'[32]
Incorporating such observations in his book out of consideration
for the new ally must later have seemed farcical based on his
experiences in North Africa.

When Rommel began an offensive in Africa, which he usually did without bothering to inform his ally in advance, there
was always a row. Rommel believed, probably correctly, that the
Italian leadership had no interest in these offensives and wanted
to delay them until Hitler decided the war elsewhere. The storm
quickly blew over, if Rommel defeated the British. Mussolini's
Foreign Minister, Galeazzo Ciano, noted in his diary that the
Italian commanders got worked up about the Germans if a
retreat was necessary, mostly because he had no consideration for
the less mobile Italian divisions in those circumstances. For them
it was proof that Rommel was a 'flop as a leader'.[33]

Also subject to change was his relationship with Mussolini, who was nominally the Supreme Commander of the Axis Armed Forces in the North African theatre of war. Ciano, who was Mussolini's son-in-law, reported in his diary that when Rommel 'who is always at the head of his attacking troops in his armoured vehicle' pushed the British out of Cyrenaica at the beginning of 1942, the 'Duce' held him up as a shining example to his generals.[34] Again, in 1942 when the Germans overran Tobruk and crossed the Egyptian border, Mussolini praised Rommel in the grandest possible terms and even laid claim to the battle plan, even though he had originally rejected it. Ciano wrote about the Duce's claims: 'He [Rommel] really was responsible for the attack, even against the opinion of the high command. Now he fears that no one either knows how or dares to exploit the success to the full. He only trusts Rommel.'[35] The Italian dictator made his claim solely because he believed the German General would grant him immortal fame with the completion of the conquest of Egypt. The 'Duce', who wanted to be seen entering Cairo on a white steed, demanded that Italians and Germans had to be represented in equal numbers at the triumphal entrance into the city. Obviously nothing came of this wish for immortal fame and the relationship between Rommel and Mussolini rapidly declined, as well as that with the Italian generals. Kesselring, the Supreme Commander South, even believed that the conflict caused 'irreparable consequences' for the entire Axis partnership.[36]

After Rommel's offensive stalled at El Alamein Mussolini became completely critical of the German Field Marshal. On 27 September 1942 Ciano wrote with a maliciously joyful undertone, 'Mussolini is convinced that he will not return. He found him physically and morally shattered.'[37] On the other hand, Rommel told Goebbels at the beginning of 1943 that

'An old tired man.' Rommel and Mussolini, October 1943.

he did 'not think much' of the Duce. He is an 'old and tired man' who is 'lacking the consistency of a clear political and military command'.[38]

None of this conflict was apparent to the Italian common soldier. He never or only rarely saw his commanders at the front line. It was well known that General Ettore Bastico, the Supreme Commander of the Axis troops in North Africa, lived in a palatial estate 2,500 kilometres behind the front line. But the same soldier saw Rommel putting himself in harm's way and eating the same rations as his troops. This was in sharp contrast to the customs of the Italian army, where officers, junior officers and enlisted personnel ate different food. This behaviour earned Rommel the respect of the Italian 'Bersaglieri', who, based on idealised memories after the war, were supposed to have called him 'Santo Rommel', among other things. Wilfried Armbruster, Rommel's interpreter in Africa, reported that Rommel received letters from Italian soldiers, which expressed their adoration for the German general. This respect did not change the fact that Rommel looked down on the common Italian infantryman because he usually made initial judgements about people based on their military capability. Regarding the soldiers of his ally, after the end in Tunisia, the Field Marshal once said to Goebbels, 'instead of throwing themselves against the English in North Africa, they sat in their holes and chanted the rosary'.[39]

The men around Rommel were also impressed by his untiring drive and enormous physical capability. He had learned from his experiences in the First World War and during the peacetime years had consistently built up his originally weak constitution with a multitude of physical activities. The result was relentless activity, remarkable given his age and even more the extremely hostile climate in the desert war. In many respects Rommel was an example for the common soldiers who served under him. Despite the sometimes inhuman demands he required of them, his troops developed a spirit of solidarity, which gave them an inner strength and allowed them to overcome numerical superiority. The soldiers' affection for Rommel showed itself when they referred to him by his Christian name in conversations amongst themselves. 'Erwin', despite being an authority figure for them, was somehow one of them. He was never at a loss when asked for advice. He always tried to 'reduce the most difficult to a simple formulation'. He could be 'bloody rough' when things did not go as he anticipated. Yet he had praise for everyone who did his duty. Supposedly nothing gave him more pleasure than chatting in the Swabian dialect with a fellow countryman. That is how the simple 'privates', who fought and survived under his command in the deserts of North Africa and the plains of France, kept him in their romanticised memories.

117

3

The Creation of Propaganda

During a dinner with Hitler at the Reich Chancellery on 22 June 1942, a satisfied Propaganda Minister Joseph Goebbels said hardly any other general was as conversant with the importance of the use of propaganda as Rommel, it was another facet of what a 'modern general' he was.[1] By taking Tobruk on the preceding day Rommel had become the perfect advertisement for Hitler's military might. The propaganda machine of the Third Reich had glorified him like no other general of the Wehrmacht and in a well-calculated programme made him into the idol of all Germans.

The Exception

The background for this rise to prominence was the seamless dovetailing of Rommel's soldierly ambition on the one hand and the goals of National Socialist propaganda on the other. The modern, unorthodox tank general, who had demonstrated superiority over the ponderous battle leadership of the French and the British, presented the system with its new type of military leader. The Nazis considered him to be a man of willpower, not much given to cool calculation. And this very determined person was able to triumph over, or at least stand up to, materially superior enemies. Such a prototype of the National Socialist army leader was useful to the Germans since he was able to suggest to them superiority and confidence in victory in equal amounts. Additionally, the propaganda surrounding the General was to be used as a 'psychological weapon' against the enemy.

Hitler recognised the value of propaganda early on. In *Mein Kampf* he praised the 'brilliant' British propaganda of the First World War and disparaged that of Imperial Germany, accusing it of being no more than 'insipid pacifist bilge' and totally incapable of 'firing men's spirits until they were willing to die'.[2] In contrast he described the Nazi propaganda machine as 'something wonderful' because it had mobilised the masses and contributed to converting the German nation into his willing instrument. Hitler considered the propaganda promotion of anyone other than himself as 'unhealthy'. This meant that photographs of army commanders and other generals could only be published with his express authorisation. The only exception was Rommel, his 'favourite general'. Goebbels' propaganda was soon to focus on him in great detail. Hitler, who had the latest weekly newsreels shown to him for his approval, helped shape the propaganda around the General. He criticised, made suggestions or even dictated new commentaries.

When Goebbels said that Rommel was a 'modern General' in the truest sense of the word, he was referring to the openness Rommel showed to the 'marketing' of his image by Nazi propaganda. Rommel correctly believed that popularity would help advance his career. The Nazis, with their feel for the importance of propaganda, made the famous 'People's Wireless Sets' popular and used aeroplanes for the first time in Hitler's election campaign trips. Rommel, who was always interested in technical developments, recognised the possibilities of the

Striking a pose. The 'Desert Fox' alone in the Libyan wastes, November 1942.

newest inventions of his time. When Rommel was in the field in France and Africa he always had a camera with him, typically one given to him by the Propaganda Minister, and made constant use of it. His photographs supposedly filled several albums, and he generously shared some of them with magazines. The cover page of the *Frankfurter Illustrierte* once showed him taking photographs from a tank, a very unusual image of a Wehrmacht general. Rommel enjoyed posing for the camera even more than he enjoyed taking photographs. Most of his fellow officers and generals commented disparagingly on the 'propaganda chaps', but Rommel practically courted the attention of the photographic and film crews of the propaganda companies, which concentrated on him like on no other general of the Wehrmacht. It has been said that the reporters attached to him were banned from writing or taking photographs when he was away from the battlefield and temporarily replaced by another commander. He often had scenes re-shot because he believed he had not been lit to his best advantage. Rommel's vanity about this was so pronounced that the propaganda companies sometimes only pretended to film the General in order to keep him in a good mood. Rommel experienced 'wonderful moments' when they captured him on celluloid, particularly after a military victory. He then proudly informed his wife that the entire scene had been filmed and would surely be seen in one of the next weekly newsreels.

Functionaries from the Berlin Ministry, who had exchanged their brown Party uniform for the field-grey of the Wehrmacht, managed the interface between the propaganda head office and the 'Panzer General'. Since they were aware of Rommel's good relationship with Hitler, they thought it would be to their advantage to be present at battles under the command of Hitler's favourite. This was particularly true for two individuals during the Western campaign; Karl Hanke, the Undersecretary of State at the Propaganda Ministry and later Gauleiter of Silesia, and Karl Holz, the editor of the Nazi hate rag *Der Stürmer*, both of whom were totally unsuited to military service. In Africa Rommel was fortunate to have as his aide-de-camp and later company commander Alfred-Ingemar Berndt, whom the former Foreign Minister Constantin von Neurath described as a 'fanatical Nazi'. Berndt was not only a callous and cunning propaganda 'manager' but also an effective direct link to Goebbels. As Ministerialdirektor of the Propaganda Ministry, Berndt was responsible for censorship of the entire Reich press. He impressed Rommel with his personal courage and in time became one of the future Field Marshal's closest confidants. Rommel frequently used Berndt as a courier between North Africa and both the Propaganda Ministry and Führer Headquarters.

The Horseman of the Apocalypse

Rommel's Panzer division stood out from the mass of Wehrmacht units deployed in the Western campaign for two main reasons. The first reason was Rommel's easy and at the same time unorthodox leadership, the second was his special relationship to propaganda. The fact that Rommel's division in General Hermann Hoth's Panzer Corps was the spearhead of General von Kluge's Fourth Army also helped. The division's breakthrough of the French lines became an immediate propaganda spectacle. However, the focus was less on Rommel than on the striking power of the new German Wehrmacht. Relevant to the concept of the 'Blitzkrieg', Hitler's tanks appeared 'fast as an arrow,' like 'horsemen of the apocalypse' or even a tornado to 'sweep over France'. 'The black devils have finished another great hunt,' a typical report in a daily paper at that time said. 'For the second time in four weeks they broke out of the centre of the German right wing, shot out, mowed down and flattened the front of the Allies with short decimating hammer blows, again stormed deep to the south, and then after a fantastic flank march at St. Valéry, triumphed and took Sedan again, as they had done at Amiens and Abbeville.'[3]

Soon the commander of the 7th Panzer Division stepped into the glaring propaganda spotlight. His leadership style added an additional component to the Blitzkrieg. Combined with the power of the tanks and the dive-bombers was the unexpectedness of his attacks. The propaganda '*matcher*' linked this with a scenario from the supernatural. The 7th Panzer was dubbed the 'Ghost Division', eerie to the opponents, led with 'ghostly daring'. Newspapers described the 'ghostly' Panzer

Division and its commander to its readers as advancing at night or in diffuse morning light, appearing unexpectedly and unbelievably far behind enemy lines, all with 'unreal graceful speed and manoeuvrability'.[4] A poem of nine stanzas was printed in a motorcycle rifle company's Swabian paper, a parody of Hans Albers' 'On the Reeperbahn at 12:30 am'. One verse read:

On the Rommelbahn at half three in the night
Ghosts race by in full might
Rommel himself is in front
Keeping up is everyone's wont
On the Rommelbahn at half three in the night.[5]

From that time on propaganda concentrated more and more on Rommel's persona. He was attributed special characteristics. For example, one could read that 'the personal motto of the Führer, "what does not defeat me only makes me stronger"', was also 'the battle cry of this Seydlitz who led here, and his daring band'.[6] In the reports, Rommel appeared hard on himself and relentless in pursuing his opponents. 'The general took care of the rest, who still expected to be saved. At the head of his Panzer troop he took his own prisoners, smiling grimly.' His leadership style was not what one called 'the old classical school in the West'. No, he represented the 'revolutionary strategy' of the Blitzkrieg. In order to set Rommel's leadership in battle apart from what had previously been the normal rules of engagement a new vocabulary was created. 'Rommeln' ('to Rommel') became the verb describing a daring advance deep into enemy territory, which so upset the enemy's static war plans.

126

'A dangerously determined chin.' Propaganda photo from 1941.

Naturally a visual image appropriate to the ideal modern general was a part of Rommel's characterisation. His portrait, whether drawing or photograph, already filled the during the Western campaign. War correspondents interpreted his image as, 'His head shows a high, smooth forehead, a strong energetic nose, prominent cheekbones, a narrow mouth with tight lips above a chin of dangerous determination. The strong lines around the nostrils and corners of his mouth would ease into smiling mischievousness. His clear and blue eyes, cool in a ponderous glance, penetrating and focused, revealed the cunning which marks this man, and if it broke though, imbued his Colleoni head with lovely warmth.'[7]

Soon reports in both national and local publications were drawing parallels between the company commander of the

First World War and the divisional commander of the Second World War. The small newssheet of the former Württemburg Mountain Battalion carried a description written by Captain Herrman Aldinger, Rommel's comrade in the First World War and later his adjutant. 'A daredevil almost more so now than 20 years ago.'[8] *Der Gebirgler* celebrated 'its Rommel' in grand style on the first page. Under the headline 'There is only one Rommel . . .' were Aldinger's words, 'You should have seen him, standing erect in a command vehicle, often completely alone in a wide open field'.[9]

The citizens of Heidenheim, Rommel's birthplace, were also proud of him. The Lord Mayor surprised soldiers from the town with a Christmas package in December 1940. The package, which was organised by local Party functionaries, contained a fir branch, cigars, Magenbrot (special Swabian cookies) and a colour postcard portrait of the dashing Major-General painted by the 'well known artist Wolf Willrich.' The portrait was intended as a morale-booster as the third year of the war was fast approaching. The postcard was accompanied by a Christmassy propaganda sheet citing a letter whose extremely superficial text held up Rommel as an example of the bravery and boldness demanded of each soldier.

'And now, my heartfelt thanks for the Rommel card. This is our general, as he lives and breathes. Hard and relentless on himself and his men, but a real man and a good comrade. It was with this face that he shot a round with a flare gun, the only available weapon, into the vision slit of a French tank, and the tank turned around. . . . That is Rommel, "our Rommel!" Now I have a request, could I have a card for each of my other comrades . . . ?' one private wrote to the sender of the Christmas package.[10]

128

A coloured postcard portrait for Christmas. The Lord Mayor of Heidenheim had it sent to sons of the city serving in the field in 1940.

The 'blessed army leader' who headed a powerful division in the structure of the victorious Wehrmacht that overran France in a matter of weeks, was superbly suited to be the star of a great feature-length propaganda film. Goebbel's ministry got busy shortly after the cessation of hostilities, and filming for the movie *Victory in the West* started as early as August 1940. It was shot in the actual locations of the battles. No trouble or expense was spared to 'show how it really was'. Rommel, whom Goebbels had personally convinced to participate, acted decisively both in front of and behind the cameras. As the leading man he crossed over the Somme and advanced to the

English Channel at the head of his 'Ghost Division' once more, and employed far too convincingly dejected extras – they were French prisoners of war – to give a realistic impression of the recently-defeated.

At the beginning of February 1941, just a year after the first showing of a movie about the Luftwaffe in the Polish campaign, *Victory in the West* premiered at the Berlin Ufa-Palast. Swastika banners and Reich war flags had been draped in front of the cinema the day before. A large Army band played as the heads of the Wehrmacht and Party joined for this great occasion. When the film subsequently opened at the other theatres in the Reich's capital the ticket offices were mobbed. People watched the film with the knowledge that Hitler had just given the 'Panzer General' a new command in North Africa.

A Modern von Lettow-Vorbeck

Rommel watched the film a few weeks later, at the beginning of March 1941, at a smaller gathering. He had invited a few Italian officers as his guests, and greeted them with the remark that one day they would be able to see a film entitled *Victory in Africa.* The film was shown in an officer's mess in Tripoli, the capital of Italy's North African colony. Rommel and the special 'aura' of Africa were linked together to increase the popularity, in the National Socialist sense, of the prototypical 'Panzer General'.

The colonial resonances of Africa allowed Rommel to appear in the eyes of many Germans as a new Colonel Paul von Lettow-Vorbeck, the famous commander of the Kaiser's army in German East Africa in the First World War. However, boosting Rommel's image was not the only aim of the exercise. When they deployed to Tripoli the German troops had set foot on another continent. In effect, Africa also symbolised a massive expansion of the German sphere of influence. The newsreels portrayed this in both romanticised scenes as well as action sequences. Pictures of palm trees bending in the wind and white minarets reaching toward the cloudless sky alternated with camel herds moving through the trackless desert. Shots of eggs frying on tank hulls, which of course actually needed to be cooked with a blowtorch, gave the illusion of a grand adventure. These romantic scenes contrasted with scenes of the tankers of the Afrika Korps rushing toward Egypt enveloped in clouds of dust, accompanied by the stirring rhythms of the specially-composed 'Song of Africa'. General Rommel was always in the lead, always at the centre of the action. No matter the occasion, he was there: in an open vehicle at the head of his Panzer division, in a field-commander pose silhouetted against the sky, observing a artillery duel with binoculars in hand, explaining new attack objectives at a map table or inspecting shot-up British tanks.

The newsreels were not alone; the war correspondents also drew a colourful picture of Africa, alternating between romanticised idyll and heroic cliché. They wrote about the 'numbing heat' of the perpetually cloudless days, the pounding Ghibli sandstorms, and the colourful blooming of the desert in the spring. The reports of Hans Freiherr von Esebeck, who accompanied Rommel for years, suggest kitschy lyricism. He wrote about the sun, which stood at the 'horizon like a milky disc in the haze of the morning clouds' and 'lifted the land slowly out of the enchantment of the night'. 'On the remote road, which stretched over soft hills like a broad glittering shoelace, lay the fort of El Agheila, a tower, bulky, thick surrounded by walls of clay and brick as if it [. . .] had been lifted from a tale in

131

'Rommel' – an old Arabic word for sand? In North Africa 1942.

The Arabian Nights. Far off in the desert dust devils played in the morning wind, and the colours of the endless plain changed from the grey of first light to the yellow of day, flashing suddenly in a myriad of twinkling dew drops in which the silhouettes of the low camel-thorn bushes looked like ink blots. Unnoticed, the sky had turned a deep blue and the edges of the distant jebel [mountains] now glittered in the brilliant rays of the unleashed sun.'[11] And, of course, always a vital part of this romantic scene: Rommel. Resourceful propaganda specialists came up with their own explanation of why he was integral to this vista. They claimed to have discovered that among the 80 or more words in Arabic for sand, one in old Arabic was 'Rommel'.[12]

By the end of March 1941 the war correspondents were able to report the usual things about Rommel from North Africa, by then the only remaining ground war after the defeat of France. The Panzer General drove to the east at the head of his under-strength units. Rommel strongly emphasised the comparison between the battle of Tobruk, the battle in the 'Carthaginian sand', with the battle of Cannae where Hannibal defeated the Romans. He, a newcomer to the desert, was arriving 2,000 years later to serve up a 'modern Cannae' to the British.[13] Rommel wrote to his wife in April 1941 that the all the world's press was talking about his success; at the same time the battle for the fortress of Tobruk was slowly descending into disaster. The forces assigned to the Afrika Korps had not been intended for such a large-scale operation and were not strong enough for the siege. A company commander in a Panzer regiment reported what the men of the Afrika Korps actually experienced under Rommel's leadership that April. He wrote about the repeated orders to attack the British troops defending Tobruk. 'The time seemed endless until we fought our way back to the breach and slowly got out of the line of fire. There is not a single fighting vehicle amongst those that have returned that does not have significant scars. We are devastated to find how many of our comrades are missing. The losses are terrible. Many a tear leaves its tracks in grey, dusty faces. . . . Our old Great War veterans claim they have never seen a blacker day.'[14] The same officer also wrote that few back home could imagine anything even approaching the truth from the highly-coloured reports of the propaganda companies. Every day in Africa was a battle against the adversities of this continent. When no sand storm was blowing swarms of flies and wretched monotony plagued the soldiers. The heat was the worst. Metal became so hot it could not be touched. 'Later back home I saw in a newsreel how soldiers fried eggs on the red-hot tank. The enjoyment in the audience over this was great; everyone thought they have it so good down there. I could have screamed with rage! Where were we supposed to get the eggs from, and particularly the fat.' In fact food was held to have been one of the worst things. Bread, leathery beef in tins or sardines in oil and dried vegetables; day after day, week after week, month after month, the same thing. 'All of which truly are not suitable photographic subjects for war reporters! So you get pictures of palm groves, oases, camels, donkeys, Arabs or pictures from Tripoli, Benghazi or Derna put in front of you and think that is our world.'[15] This is precisely what happened in the spring months of 1941. The first crisis for the Wehrmacht since the start of the war was covered up with pretty pictures and talk of great successes. The enormous territorial gains, totally meaningless in a desert war, made the cover-up easy because Rommel had advanced almost 1,000 kilometres.

Many people, basing their impression on the portrait of him drawn by propaganda, thought that it was the proper moment to erect a 'biographical monument' to Rommel. 'I want to create a work of lasting value that shows the character of the young general of our time, presents him as an example for future generations and thus creates a starting point for soldierly enthusiasm and improvement again,' was the offer of a colonel to the much-lauded General.[16] In foreign countries people gradually began to take notice of Rommel and requested information about the general who had consolidated his position even after the crisis at Tobruk and had dealt the British a serious defeat near the Egyptian border at Sollum in mid-June during a three-day tank battle. The Propaganda Ministry in Berlin was happy to oblige. It created a suitable National Socialist CV for Rommel, which the weekly newspaper *Das Reich* printed in April 1941. This claimed Rommel was a son of the working classes who had left the army after the First World War to study at Tübingen University. As one of the first SA leaders he was supposed to have received National Socialist insights through his personal relationship with Hitler.

Back in North Africa, Rommel was receiving fan mail by the sackful. However when he read his 'life story' he became quite upset at how high-handedly the propaganda machine had appropriated his history. He did not understand that he was their creation. So far he had only profited from the propaganda, but now for the first time he realised the drawbacks of his being 'marketed'. He angrily wrote 'nonsense' in large letters in the margin of the article. His adjutant mentioned this episode in a letter to Lucie Rommel shortly afterwards, telling her he had already spoken with Berndt on the subject. He said all of Germany knew of Rommel's great merits and there was no reason to make up untruthful statements about him. However, Rommel himself even took action. As direct as he was guileless, he asked the Propaganda Ministry in Berlin what they were thinking of with this article. He was referred to the author of the article, a certain Alfred Tschimpke, who had already written a book about the 7th Panzer Division in the French campaign and several newspaper reports on Rommel's Africa 'expedition'. Rommel indignantly confronted Tschimpke, who denied that he had written the false biography and at the same time asked the Propaganda Ministry why they had put him in such a bad spot. A Dr Otto Meisner from the Overseas Department of the Reich Press Office, answered him somewhat later. He expressed the opinion that the contents of the article about Rommel could hardly harm the reputation of such an excellent man. On the contrary, it would increase his popularity in foreign countries. Meissner's cynical closing remark indicated

Rommel's role as a propaganda object when he stated that perhaps it would have been good from a propaganda perspective if Rommel's actual career had corresponded to the details provided by the Reich. In fact Rommel had never belonged to either the SA or the Nazi Party.

Naturally Goebbels was not concerned about Rommel's reaction. By the spring of 1941, he had virtually 'hammered' the name 'Rommel' as a synonym for the invincibility of the German Wehrmacht into the public consciousness with both words and images. For the general population, which Goebbels handled with the total contempt he held for any manipulable mass, 'Africa' and 'Rommel' ('The Lord of the Desert War' as the war correspondent von Esebeck liked to call him) had gradually become interchangeable terms.

The Diversionary Tactic

After the headline-poor summer months, the newspaper *Völkische Beobachter* featured Rommel, accompanied by a photo of him wearing a pith helmet, as 'an exemplary soldierly manifestation of a revolutionary nation' in honour of his 50th birthday on 15 November 1941. This heralded the start of a new propaganda campaign starring the General, but the objective had now changed. Starting in the late autumn of 1941, the National Socialist propaganda emphasis on Rommel in North Africa was designed to distract attention from the precarious situation on the Russian Front.

When the Russian campaign started on 22 June 1941, the day before the anniversary of Napoleon's invasion in 1812, Germany's entire propaganda machine focussed on Russia. Goebbels intended to make the anticipated quick victory into a great propaganda spectacle. The great expectations for the Blitzkrieg seemed to have been fulfilled during the first weeks of 'Operation Barbarossa'. Despite sympathy for Rommel, the action in North Africa was therefore pushed into the background. 'At the moment we are only stepchildren and have to make the best of it. Doesn't matter, they are making good progress in Russia and our time will come again,' Rommel wrote at the end of September 1941.[17]

Beginning in December when the Russian winter had begun and the Soviets had launched massive counter-offensives, the Propaganda Ministry began to realise the German High Command had miscalculated. The attention of the German nation, now focussed with great concern on the battlefields of Russia, had to be diverted. The catastrophe which had befallen the German army in the east required compensation. What could be more obvious for the propaganda strategists at this moment than to counterbalance the war on the ice-cold Russian Front with the clashes in hot Africa? Goebbels had already felt there had not been enough coverage of Rommel's 50th birthday. On 28 November 1941, he urgently advised Generals Keitel and Jodl of the OKW to do something 'to elevate [Rommel] to a kind of national hero,' since he had more or less disappeared from public view. Goebbels insisted that the Army needed this as the Navy and Air Force also had their own heroes. For whatever reason, the generals agreed with the suggestion of the powerful propaganda chief; they were in 'extraordinary' agreement, even, as Goebbels noted in his diary.[18]

The propaganda machine had to wait before it could concentrate on Africa and Rommel because in mid-November 1941 the British had launched a great surprise offensive. In the course of the subsequent battles, which the British compared to

Blenheim and Waterloo, Rommel was forced back in an orderly retreat. By the end of 1941 he was able to withdraw intact to where he had started his offensive a few months earlier, the Great Syrte west of El Agheila. But when Rommel began efforts in January 1942 to recapture the lost terrain the propaganda finally had its chance to 'turn around'. Goebbels viewed this as critical since the 'German *Volksgenossen*' had become aware of the catastrophic situation on the Eastern Front.

The newsreels began reporting with increasing frequency from North Africa. The films masterfully gave Rommel's advance a significance which it did not really have. The editing of these newsreels indicated how seriously Germans were to view this secondary theatre of war. Reports from the fronts in the West and, starting in June 1941, the East started off by showing general maps of the situation. By contrast, the importance of the campaign in Africa was emphasised by its title given in large white letters on a background of the entire black continent. What followed was the second round in the transfiguration of the 'Panzer General' and his African mission.

War correspondents now interwove the *gestalt* of Rommel with almost esoteric drivel: 'In the room's twilight he suddenly was standing in front of me – a meteor always on its flight path in important mission … aglow with sacred enthusiasm … being so close to reality prevents one from understanding such an occurrence and transforms it into an equation or a parable so it can jump into the minds and hearts as an immortal legend as his personality and actions are standing before us exemplarily – we are still missing the religion of newly generally applicable measure to which figure could be – so to speak Polykletically – be inserted into the measurement of a holy geometry [*sic*]', *Schwäbische Zeitung* wrote.[19]

A break at the Egyptian border. Cover page of the Party magazine from July 1941.

139

Even the magazine of the German airforce operating in the Mediterranean, *Adler im Süden* ('Eagle of the South'), dedicated a cover story to the 'great general'. This was printed only on Goebbels' orders; the Luftwaffe staff were not enamoured of Rommel. In their eyes he took all the credit for his successes without mentioning the importance of their part in the hard fighting. The article established a link between Rommel and the great army leaders of the past. 'What would Sedan have been without Moltke, Tannenberg without Hindenburg, Waterloo without Blücher and Gneisenau . . . what would the fight in North Africa be without the brilliant fencing artistry of General Rommel?' He was elevated to this exclusive circle of Prussian military greats and finally became the 'Executor of the Will of History'.[20]

By the end of 1941 Rommel had also become the German general best known to the British public, one to whom they paid a certain respect. Rommel had already wrung grudging praise and almost daily headlines from the British press during his retreat. The war correspondent of the *Daily Express*, Alan Moorehead, wrote: 'You really have to have been there to see these retreats. They were repeatedly interrupted by deadly accurate counter attacks and flying tank columns were constantly blocking our advance. The claim that the Germans are beaten once they start to retreat is dangerous nonsense. It is a disservice to the British troops to repeat such rubbish even nowadays. Rommel's general staff has never made the mistake of under-estimating us.'[21]

Even Auchinleck, who replaced General Archibald Wavell as Supreme Commander of the British forces in the Middle East in June 1941 after the British defeat at Sollum, found some words of respect for his enemy, whom he said took advantage of opportunities offered him 'in a brilliant manner'. The fact that Rommel was able to repeatedly evade encirclement by British forces despite a massive sandstorm around Agedabia was emphasised. The British were not quite ready to celebrate yet. Instead their generals and the press began to embrace the heroic image fostered by Goebbels.

A Superman

It was unsurprising that two days after the start of the Rommel's offensive in January 1942 the United Press news agency reported from London: 'One must admit that General Rommel has again proven his art of leadership in battle'.[22] On the following day General Auchinleck wrote to Churchill that the enemy had 'unexpectedly' been able to continue his advance and this had temporarily brought disorder to his own forces. 'Once again Rommel's clever move has succeeded,' Auchinleck indicated. Churchill responded asking helplessly, 'I find the report from the Eighth Army, which speaks of withdrawing from Benghazi and Derna, very disturbing. I certainly have been given no reason to expect the development of such a situation. It seems to me we are in a serious crisis, which I have in no manner anticipated. Why is everyone retreating so rapidly?'[23]

Shortly thereafter the Reuters press agency reported that according to statements in military circles the initiative in Libya had passed into Rommel's hands. Churchill needed to find an explanation for the House of Commons as to why this Rommel had been able to reverse a situation in North Africa where the British had seemed to be in control. Of course Churchill did not want to publicly admit that he did not have enough troops there; it had been necessary to redeploy British

141

units to the Far East after the Japanese declaration of war. In order to justify British reverses in North Africa he found it useful to portray the German general as a virtual superman. They were dealing with an 'extraordinarily bold and clever opponent, a great field commander', if he was allowed to say that 'despite and beyond the horrors of war', Churchill said in the Commons[24] and thereby created the basis for Rommel's popularity even amongst his enemies.

The United States, on which Hitler had declared war on 11 December 1941, had also taken notice of the 'rascal among generals', as one American radio commentator called him. It was said there that many great soldiers, great leaders and commanders had been developed in the struggles in North Africa. And they further noted that if the whole great drama was to have one unique hero, then it would be Rommel. The extraordinary, almost mythical hold the German 'Panzer General' seemed to have on his opponents was also talked about in the United States. 'The British 8th Army idolises him. They admire him because he beat them and were surprised to have beaten in turn such a capable general,' the observers from the other side of the Atlantic said.[25]

Churchill's promotion of Rommel's reputation in the western media did a disservice to the British troops fighting in the North African desert. Just the name Rommel alone was having a devastating effect on their morale. Rommel became a psychological problem for them, and apparently the soldiers' effectiveness suffered to such an extent that General Auchinleck felt a need to counter this energetically. He drafted a circular to all commanders and chiefs of staff that was as impressive as it was indicative of the spiritual climate and psychological condition of the troops in the North African theatre of war at the beginning

142

Always out in front. Rommel at the machine gun of an armoured reconnaissance vehicle.

of 1942. It said that there was a real danger that 'our friend Rommel' was becoming a 'sort of sorcerer or bogeyman for our troops' because they talked about him too much. He was certainly no superman, despite the fact that he was really very energetic and capable. 'But even if he were a superman, it remains highly undesirable that our men ascribe supernatural powers to him. I require you to use all available means to get rid of the perception once and for all that Rommel represents something more than a normal general and in fact a very unpleasant one as we know from the mouths of our own officers. The main issue is to ensure that Rommel is not always referred to when we mean the enemy. We have to make reference to "the Germans" or to "the forces of the Axis" or to "the enemy" and not always emphasise Rommel. Take note that this order should be followed promptly and all commanders are advised

*Styled as a superman
even by the enemy.
Rommel in his
command vehicle, 1942.*

that this matter is of utmost importance from a psychological
perspective.' It is significant that Auchinleck closed his circular
with the comment that he was not jealous of Rommel.[26]

Meanwhile Rommel was thrilled with the worldwide
admiration he was receiving. According to a Gallup Poll he
was the best-known German in foreign countries in 1942 after
Hitler. This flattered his vanity. 'The opinion of me in the world
press has improved,' he wrote to his wife in January 1942.[27]
Goebbels could also be satisfied. He happily wrote in his diary
at the beginning of 1942, 'Rommel continues to be the recognised darling of even the enemies' news agencies. He has truly
become a ghost general. Today he is as well known in the USA
as in London or Berlin, one of the few figures in the German
Army to enjoy a worldwide reputation.'[28]

On the subject of General Douglas MacArthur he said
that he was being transformed into a Hollywood general. 'I
am having the gentleman shown by his true colours. The

Americans are trying to turn him into the greatest general of the war. In reality he has no more to show in the way of heroic deeds and performance than a relatively brief resistance on Corregidor and an ignominious flight. What could the Americans achieve if they had a Dietl or Rommel!!! One can see just how humble we still are in our propagandistic tendencies . . .'[29] Just how convinced Goebbels was of the effectiveness of the propaganda 'weapon' was demonstrated in his observation that fear of Rommel was ubiquitous in Great Britain. This general was being seen as a legendary figure. That he managed to tie down some British forces was seen as being almost miraculous. It showed what the initiative, courage and imagination of a fighting general had to offer in the end, in spite of disadvantageous conditions.

The propaganda stir over Rommel, strengthened by participation from foreign countries, undeniably had a strong impact on him. The 'Panzer General' set his goals even higher. At the beginning of 1942, his reputation in the Reich, racing ahead of him, started to take on a life of its own. The Reich Press Chief Dr Otto Dietrich realised this and felt compelled to put 'the brakes on' the aura that had become associated with Rommel's name. He achieved this by using one of the so-called 'Tagesparolen'. These were daily instructions, approved by Hitler, on language to be used for reporting news from the various fronts. At the end of January 1942 he determined that 'a careful watch should be kept on internal German propaganda so no false military hopes are raised'. For example, this applied to actual successes in Libya, which should be prevented from being presented as a prelude to the re-conquest of Cyrenaica.[30]

At the beginning of February Rommel had actually taken Cyrenaica. He had 'pulled the rabbit out of the hat again', as one American radio reporter expressed it. The waves of adulation in the press rose even higher. The *Times* made Rommel the subject of a lead article, and *The Observer* dedicated a biographical sketch to him. While the subject of all this praise paused in the spring of 1942, holding his positions, the war correspondents stuck to his heels. The reports, often illustrated, whether 'In the Bunkers at Tobruk' or 'With General Rommel on Patrol', were published in big spreads, and sometimes even serialised in the dailies and magazines.

The Reich Press Chief felt he needed to urge constraint again, even when Cyrenaica, with its ports of Benghazi and Derna, had been won back for the Axis. He could not allow a 'hothouse atmosphere' to develop over successes in North Africa. The situation had to be calmly and factually reported in the press. It would be a great mistake to present the nation with goals that could not be achieved. He prohibited 'using the words "Suez Canal" at all in the press' when reporting on the recapture of Cyrenaica.[31] It is clear the underlying intent of this edict was to rein in the widespread optimism that Rommel would, as one naval newssheet put it, 'solve even superhuman tasks' on the precarious flank of the Axis and take Egypt from the British.[32]

Conquering Egypt was exactly what Rommel had in mind when he launched his decisive campaign at the end of May 1942. Barely a month later Tobruk, which had defied a months-long siege the previous year, fell to the Afrika Korps. This was the 'keystone', the supposed last bastion of resistance on the road to Cairo and the Suez Canal. The propaganda company's photographers stuck to Rommel's heels right through the final phase of the battle. Even before the British surrender he spoke a few well-chosen words into the microphone of the war correspondent of the Grossdeutschen Rundfunk (Greater

One of many headlines. The *Völkischer Beobachter* of 22 June 1942.

German Radio, the official state radio). They were quickly transmitted to Berlin, which broadcast them into German living rooms the following evening. While the photographers were still filming Rommel in a heroic pose on the summit of a hill overlooking Tobruk or standing on a tank, victory fanfares were being broadcast on Greater German Radio. In a frenetic voice the newsreader announced Rommel's capture of the long and hard-fought fortress of Tobruk.

The ensuing headlines of this and the following day went overboard. Huge letters emblazoned 'Rommel's Glorious Victory' across the front page of the *Völkischer Beobachter.*[33] The Army Commander was celebrated as 'The Hero of Acroma and Tobruk' in the *Chemnitzer Tageszeitung.*[34] A common feature of these reports was that they described the fall of Tobruk using phrases such as 'it took the breath away' of the British or stabbed them 'in the middle of the heart.' They claimed it was a greater shock to them than Dunkirk or the fall of Singapore.

147

They talked of a stunned British public and Churchill at a loss. Actually the Prime Minister had been informed of the surrender while at a reception by the American president at the White House. He was thrown into consternation because he had personally intervened to make sure British propaganda had especially featured the defence of Tobruk.

The topic of 'Rommel' was the centre of conversation during luncheon in the Reich Chancellery the day after the surrender. Goebbel's masterful product had reached the pinnacle of his glory. The Propaganda Minister incessantly praised the man Hitler had promoted to Field Marshal, and of course indirectly the success of his propaganda strategy to distract attention from the Russian crisis. He said that, 'generals like von Brauchitsch, Rundstedt and so on do not enjoy Rommel's popularity by any means . . . . When the press is silent about men like von Brauchitsch, Rundstedt and so on the public will no longer speak about them.' Rommel, on the other hand, already commanded such a reputation that his name 'has become in the minds of our population the personification of the successful German soldier'. Hitler also remarked that Rommel being so much the centre of attention was also thanks to the British, who produced an unbelievable amount of propaganda about him. The British leadership must have hoped 'to be able to explain their defeat to their own nation more easily by focusing on Rommel'.[35] Hitler was doubtless correct about this. A few days later he pointed in particular to Churchill's speeches in the Commons, 'in which, for political reasons, Rommel is repeatedly presented as a general with genius-like capabilities.' But Hitler thought he detected other motives on the part of his opponent. 'Churchill is naturally doing this so he does not have to admit the British are receiving a thrashing by the

Italian soldiers in Libya and Egypt. Maybe he also hopes to foster discord between the Italians and us by emphasising Rommel. The Duce, though, is far too sensible not to be able to see through this manoeuvre. Consequently he has acknowledged Rommel's achievements many times to the world. As a result of Churchill's actions and the Duce's acceptance, Rommel's name has attained an unimaginable respect among the primitive nations of North Africa and the Near East. This fact shows how dangerous it is to put so much emphasis on a capable opponent's man as Churchill has done in the case of Rommel. A name suddenly begins to acquire a meaning this way that is equal in value to several divisions.'[36]

As Rommel had broken off, to quote the *Völkischer Beobachter* in its 22 June 1942 issue, the 'last and most important corner post of the British defence system' with the capture of Tobruk, Goebbels obviously once again feared that the dynamic associated with Rommel's name would regain momentum. There were virtually no doubts in the Reich any more that Rommel would now take Egypt and break the British Empire apart. Therefore on the following day the Propaganda Minister directed press and radio broadcasters that the fall of Tobruk 'should not be allowed to create the impression in the German public that England was already on its knees.'[37]

In spite of Goebbels the propaganda did developed its own dynamic. Kesselring spoke of a 'Victory Psychosis'[38], which also infected Hitler and surely contributed to his allowing the North Africa offensive to continue, despite his earlier agreement to attack Malta. He wrote to the Duce, who was already planning his triumphal entry into Cairo, in a style totally consistent with the prevailing propaganda. 'The goddess of battle luck only passes by the field commanders once. He who does not seize the moment will often never be able to catch up with her.'[39] Rommel grabbed for her. That he would also hold on to her seemed beyond question, a view the propaganda promoted most of all.

Whilst the newsreels in German cinemas were reporting the victory at Tobruk with an unprecedented level of detail, the Field Marshal's offensive was already running into difficulties. Consequently commentators – making no mention of the word 'Egypt ' – limited themselves to reporting that Rommel knew no rest. 'The fight must go on,' Rommel was quoted to have said. It did continue, but the tide of war was beginning to turn. As the situation began to deteriorate the use of Rommel as a propaganda weapon became all the more important. When the sick and exhausted Field Marshal, after two futile attempts to penetrate the El Alamein defences, spent a holiday in the Reich, Goebbels presented him at an international news conference, staged just for him. Given the situation in North Africa the event in early October 1942 had a twofold purpose: Rommel was supposed to spread optimism, necessary because the German war leadership was not producing results anywhere else. At the same time his appearance was to counter rumours of his severe illness, which had spread after enemy intelligence had intercepted a radio message to that effect.

Goebbels could not have staged Rommel's appearance before the representatives of the international press more effectively. Everyone's eyes were turned to the army commander; the film cameras were whirring. Placing his hand symbolically on a door handle, Rommel triumphantly declared, 'Today we stand 100 kilometres from Alexandria and Cairo and have the gates of Egypt in hand, and with the intent to act!'[40] After this bit of drama he gave a short speech. All the foreign journalists were

The show Field Marshal. Rommel as the celebrated hero at the Berlin Sportpalast, September 1942.

favourably impressed. The representative of the *Svenska Dagbladet* reported to his readers the following day that one had to imagine not an old warhorse but a clever, superior and thoughtful man. (Rommel was very sensitive to accusations from his critics that he was a risk-taker.) This man, thanks to his unusual determination and athletic ability, was able to spur his men to great achievements and endure the greatest stresses to which he as a commanding officer could be exposed. When Goebbels asked him about his personal leadership style Rommel answered that naturally he did not put himself in danger unnecessarily but that in modern war a commander had to be in the centre of the action during the decisive phase of a battle. Seconds counted when the right orders had to be given. This was a subtle attack both on the methods of his

British opponents and the officers of the Wehrmacht General Staff and OKH.

Naturally the German propaganda machine played up Rommel's successful appearance. It sold the press conference to the public as 'being with one of the most prominent personalities of our time'. During the question and answer game between the press representatives and the Field Marshal, his 'enjoyment of the riposte, the crossing of swords' was noticeable. Goebbels, who said of the General that 'his facial expressions and his entire appearance breathe the greatness of a true personality',[41] was himself fascinated by his propaganda creation. The dashing General had been the guest of the limping little man and his large family several times during his stays in Berlin. Like Hitler, Goebbels understood how to cleverly flatter him and encourage him to stay on course. During his visit in the autumn of 1942 he used newsreel films of Rommel's victorious battles in North Africa. The Propaganda Minister's diaries indicate this ploy was successful. Rommel's mood was supposed to have improved abruptly. He clearly demonstrated this by giving spellbinding accounts that were enthusiastically absorbed by Goebbels and his family.

The British considered the first days after the fall of Tobruk as fateful. All indications were that the days of British colonial rule on the Nile were coming to an end. On Wednesday, 1 July 1942 the *Daily Mail* opened with the headline, '100 Miles From Alexandria – Rommel Pushes On 30 Miles Since Monday'. It claimed in the article that if he advanced at the same speed he would surely reach Cairo by nightfall. The situation for the British troops was extremely perilous, and as a consequence Churchill, on whom the cult of Rommel had left its mark, arrived in Cairo three days later. Sir Ian Jacob, a close confidante of the Prime Minister, reported in his diary (a report which

EIN HÄNDEDRUCK DER SIEGESGEWISSHEIT

*The 'Führer's generals'
had to be winning types.
On the cover page of the
Hamburger Illustrierte,
October 1942.*

Churchill later cited in his own memoirs), 'the Prime Minister
has only one concern . . . to beat Rommel. . . . He paced up and
down, determined to have his way and cried out, "Rommel,
Rommel, Rommel, Rommel! Does anything else count except
beating him?"'[42]

Churchill relieved Auchinleck and gave Montgomery command of the British Eighth Army in the hope that the third
general to face Rommel, after Wavell and Auchinleck, would
finally have success over the Field Marshal. Churchill shared
his reasoning with his deputy in the Office of the Prime
Minister, 'only the necessity to make a sudden, radical change
in the command leadership against Rommel and to instil confidence in the army so that a new beginning is made' caused
him to change the supreme commander.[43]

The psychological effects of the Rommel cult were wide-spread. Montgomery believed his assignment to be a personal confrontation with the opponent who up to now, despite inferior resources, had repeatedly brought the British to their knees. To constantly remind him of the challenge Montgomery hung a photograph of Rommel in his command vehicle. Montgomery's biographer, the former British Foreign Secretary Alun Chalfont, tells us he did so 'because he believed he had to understand the character of the man who was a demi-god to his own army'.[44] The relief of the British public was immense when Montgomery's successful offensive raised the siege of Egypt. The *Daily Mail*'s headline on 5 November 1942 reflects the release of their long-suppressed emotions. 'Rommel Retreats in Disorder' screamed the triumphant headline. The Afrika Korps, 'the pride of the German army', was to be pursued 'relentlessly'. One general even suggested to Churchill that he should have the church bells rung throughout the land.

The Bearer of Hope

The Security Service of the SS reported in early November 1942 that thoroughly dismantling the invincible 'monument' created by enemy propaganda served no purpose, as the public's interest was entirely focussed on the battles in North Africa. Tagesparolen of 5 and 6 November issued by the Reich Press Chief speak for themselves. In the first he urgently warned the press and broadcast media to exercise extreme restraint in their treatment of the battles in North Africa. British special announcements and reports of victories should be ignored. On the following day he issued the edict 'not to allow any appearance of pessimism to leak to the outside in these critical days'. He went further and expressed the hope 'that Field Marshal Rommel will again master the situation, as so often before.'[45] When this directive was applied to an article, the following prose emerged, 'For the Tunisian Arabs, who are fatalists and do not believe in coincidence, therefore there is no doubt – Rommel, the Sand, the almighty master of the desert, can only win. The pictorial thinking of these people gets support from the eponymous name Rommel, which enables strong flights of fancy. In a sense, the Arab has known "Rommel" and his power for thousands of years. Now it is Rommel who keeps disaster distant from Tunisia and brings freedom to the great sister nation, Egypt.'[46] All the stops were pulled out in this propaganda artistry. The German masses, who only knew Rommel as a conquering hero, were told: 'As long as Rommel is down there in Africa, nothing can happen to us,' was the general tenor of feeling in the Reich. A cartoon published in March 1943 in the *Daily Mail* shows the effect Rommel continued to have on the enemy, despite the British success in pushing the Panzerarmee Afrika into a shrinking beachhead at Tunis. Four respected Allied generals are shown in the cartoon using all their combined strength to remove Rommel who is clinging firmly to the door handle of 'Hotel Tunis'.

No one in Germany knew that the ill and depressed Rommel had already relinquished control of the 'door handle' of Africa by this time. Goebbels had decided that it would be difficult to explain to the German nation that Rommel was no longer on the scene in North Africa. As a result the Propaganda Minister had the Wehrmacht High Command announce at the beginning of May 1943 that Rommel was on a two-month convalescent leave. He knew the battles in North Africa were coming to a close and the situation demanded action. In view

'Very valuable for the future leadership of the war.' Rommel with
Propaganda Minister Joseph Goebbels.

of the fact that everyone assumed the Field Marshal was still
in Africa, he realised the government would lose credibility if
the truth were learned only after the catastrophe had occurred.
Additionally Goebbels, like Hitler, placed particular importance
on distancing Rommel from the end of operations in North
Africa. Associating Rommel with the fall of North Africa was
to be avoided at all costs because 'it would be very harmful to
his name'. This 'name' was 'very valuable' in the eyes of the
Propaganda Minister not only because of his future value in
leading the war effort but also because, as he noted in his diary,
'a military reputation such as Rommel's cannot be created and
eliminated at will'.[47]

The consequence of this decision was that someone else sent
the last radio message from Tunisia. It was the Commander of

the Afrika Korps, General Hans Cramer. The words he sent through the airwaves at 0:45am, 12 May 1943 were: 'Ammunition used up, weapons and equipment destroyed. The D.A.K. has fought per orders to the point where it can fight no more. The German Afrika Korps will rise again. Heia Safari!'[48] The propaganda strategists in Berlin went about trying to sell the defeat in Africa as really a victory for the Germans. The North African campaign was pictured as a ploy to tie down strong enemy forces, making a landing on the continent impossible and thus giving the Axis Powers time to turn Europe into an impregnable fortress. It was advertised that the father of this success was the recuperating Field Marshal Rommel. He met with Goebbels and Berndt several times in early May 1943 to work out the details of the final radio programme, '27 Months' Battle in Africa.'[49] On 12 May 1943 Rommel read with a great sense of satisfaction the yarn spun by Berndt, formerly his aide-de-camp and now once again in charge of watching over the press in the Reich. He reported how Rommel's genius, despite inferior numbers, could withstand the strength of British Empire for 27 months; how the war wrote Rommel's name on the first page of the history of the desert war, how the Master of Wartime Ruses fooled his opponent with 'Rommel Panzers' (cardboard dummies on Volkswagen chassis) and 'Rommel positions'; how he arranged 'devil's gardens' (thick land mine belts) for the defence; how he broke out of the mountains in the pouring rain like a thunderstorm to surprise the enemy and rout an Indian division with only a few hundred men; how he seized Marsa Matru in a *coup de main*; how the 'creative strategist' received his Field Marshal's baton from Hitler's hand on a sunny autumn day; how the soldiers followed his example with *élan* and fighting spirit; how he played cat and mouse with the 'Tommies.' In dramatic tones Berndt convinced the listeners of all this and more. He finally ended with the words, 'The battle is over. The flag of the famous German Afrika Korps, the flag under which the divisions that joined us later also fought, that flag has not been furled. The battalions and regiments are once again growing. They carry on the old tradition. And there will come a day when we can again sing our old battle song with pride, "the chains are rattling, the motor is droning, tanks are rolling in Africa."'[50] Rommel gratefully noted that Berndt was once again in his element, and sent the propaganda 'manager' a case of cigars.

The *cliché* of palms and adventure, in short of 'Heia Safari', continued to live on in varied forms after the capitulation in Tunisia. For example a coffee-table book was published in 1943 about the Afrika Korps. Its title was similar to the first line in Berndt's radio programme, *Swastika Over the Desert Sands*. The capture of Tobruk had provided the impetus for its publication. The book contained strong echoes of colonial times, just as had the newsreels at the time. The black native trader sits in the shade of a palm tree; a German soldier buys from him. The pilot explains everything worth knowing about a 'Messerschmidt' to a Bedouin family riding by on camels. Aircrews in uniform and natives in exotic national dress barter. Arabs invite German soldiers to share a bowl of strong Arabic coffee. Little Suleika is on the telephone for the first time. 'Brown kibitzers', native children, curiously watch a lineman from the Signal Corps at work. Natives admire German weapons and, once again, the Field Marshal, in khaki uniform, covered in dust, arm upraised, leading his tanks in attack.

The Rommel of this image now only existed in sphere of propaganda. The actual Rommel was a depressed man who was having a difficult time processing his defeat in North Africa. 'He must be a broken man due to the extended time in Africa. But one cannot let this fact become public because Rommel is, after all, the war idol of the Germans,' Goebbels wrote in his diary.[51] In the minds of the Germans hope and perseverance were firmly associated with Rommel. Once more Rommel was to give his countrymen hope. He was assigned to the Atlantic Wall, which von Rundstedt, Commander-in-Chief West, described as just a 'propaganda wall'. The Germans were given hope because Rommel had extensive experience fighting against the British and Americans. Hitler believed that against them his name alone was worth several divisions. His fast and mobile style in battle had pushed the British commanders into a corner repeatedly; the enemy troops feared him. Their fighting spirit suffered from the superman portrait propaganda had drawn. The Germans trusted him. In France, whose population was well acquainted with the Field Marshal through Vichy newsreels, he was considered to be the most capable German leader. People recognised and hailed him by name on his journeys throughout Occupied France.

During this period a propaganda unit constantly accompanied his staff. Rommel knew how much he owed it. During a journey through the Pyrenees he called a halt and photographers captured his 'field commander look', aimed at the enemy, in front of the imposing mountain scene. 'When the photo is published, the British will realise . . . that Rommel has even been to the Pyrenees.'[52] Beyond that the propaganda unit did not have much to work with until May 1944, but then Rommel expressed his confidence about the outcome of the impending 'decisive battle' in the West in an address to assembled delegations of all sections of the Wehrmacht at the

'Atlantic Base' south of Le Touquet. 'I am convinced,' he said, rising to the expectations of his position, 'that every single German soldier will make his contribution in retaliation against the Anglo-American spirit that it deserves for its criminal and bestial air war campaign against our homeland.'[53]

The newsreel cameras dutifully recorded his propaganda speech, which had the desired effect in the Reich. His words, joined with the public's faith in the Field Marshal's abilities, caused a small upsurge of optimism once again. The secret morale report by the Security Service could 'hardly detect . . . a fear of invasion.' The speech created the belief that the German nation was anticipating the great new battle as 'the last opportunity to turn over a new leaf'. After the beginning of the invasion reports from Breslau, Kiel and Coblenz indicated that 'the confidence in Rommel is great.' And as late as 25 June 1944 it was still claimed that there were 'expressions of confidence in our leadership, in particular of Field Marshal Rommel'.[54]

Taking into account Rommel's continuing positive impact on the population in an extremely tense situation, and the military and psychological 'capital' associated with his name on the battlefield, it is understandable why the Propaganda Ministry hid his serious injury of 17 June 1944. Rommel's aide-de-camp Lang noted that 'apparently . . . the name of the OB is to be exploited as a military asset', to make the world believe he still continued to be involved in the command of the battles in France.[55] Goebbels had secretly long feared this type of injury due to Rommel's front-line leadership style. At the beginning of May 1942 Rommel was almost captured in a surprise British commando raid and Goebbels noted in his diary, 'Rommel is very foolhardy with his life and safety. It would unquestionably be a national disaster if he fell into the hands of the English. He would be well advised to move about with greater care. In any event I will ensure such an event would be kept from the German nation; it would create a great disquiet.'[56]

Despite all efforts at concealment, rumours about Rommel's injury leaked out to the British press. There was even speculation that he might have died. To dispel the rumours the Propaganda Ministry required Rommel to appear in public. At his final press conference on 1 August 1944 in Paris, he exposed himself to the flashbulb storm of the photographers. On 3 August the German press issued a report that claimed Rommel had been injured in an automobile accident. Rommel 'decisively' rejected these propaganda games, playing on his image of invulnerability. He entered in his diary, that apparently it was impossible to believe that a Supreme Commander of an Army Group could be lost to ground-attack aircraft. Up until then Rommel had only seen one side of the propaganda effort, the one which accelerated his rise to Field Marshal, which brought him into favour with the great men of the Reich, helped him gain respect not only with his own people but also with people of other countries. Now in the summer of 1944 Erwin Rommel realised how much the propaganda machine had been using him. It now dropped him since a wounded, depressed Field Marshal was no longer useful as a symbol of German perseverance and confidence in victory. It was an irony of fate that Goebbel's propaganda, which had made the Field Marshal into the most popular soldier in the Reich, would allow him to become a factor in the plans of the conservative-military resistance against Hitler.

4

The Victim

R ommel had sworn the 'sacred oath to God' that he 'would give Hitler, the Commander-in-Chief of the Wehrmacht, unconditional obedience and be prepared as a brave soldier to give [his] life at anytime for this oath.'[1] The loyalty to Hitler expressed in this oath became the guiding rule in all soldierly matters for members of the Wehrmacht, with very few exceptions. The oath, which they had given on 2 August 1934, the day of Hindenburg's death, was the spontaneous idea of the then Reichswehr Minister, von Blomberg. It committed them to unconditional obedience to the State as embodied in Hitler, and even though they eventually realised that his course would lead to the demise of the Reich, the loyalty that the oath required weighed so heavily on them that the majority of soldiers, officers and generals continued to believe themselves bound by it. The Field Marshals of the Reich were required to sign yet another loyalty oath to Hitler at the beginning of March 1944. Rommel signed as a matter of course, as did von Rundstedt, Manstein and the others, although he considered this reaffirmation of the oath to Hitler as unmilitary because he believed the unconditional loyalty of an officer was a given. Only a few considered disassociating themselves from it, and several of these men decided to remove the dictator. But they

'An oath remains an oath, particularly in hopeless situations.' The Field Marshal at the Atlantic Wall, spring 1944.

failed and fell victim to his gruesome revenge. General Blumentritt, Chief of Staff to the Supreme Commander West in 1944, wrote after the war that he respected his dead comrades of 20 July but could not change his own personal decision to respect the oath! 'An oath is an oath and remains an oath, especially in impossible, hopeless situations, to prove its worth.'[2]

Rommel would probably have agreed with him had he survived the war. To break his oath and commit treason against the man who had elevated him to Field Marshal simply did not fit with his conception of loyalty. As late as the autumn of 1944, just weeks after the attempted assassination, the Field Marshal had said to a relative that Hitler was the supreme warlord and he (Rommel), as an officer, had to obey him. Nevertheless this would not prevent him from openly giving Hitler his opinion, as he had always done. At a meeting at Führer Headquarters near Soissons fourteen days after the Allied invasion the Field Marshal had pointed out to Hitler that the war in the West could not be won and a political solution had to be found. At the Berghof on 29 June and in writing on 15 July, just five days before the assassination attempt, he had presented his position in unambiguous terms. Even after 20 July Rommel, who had been seriously wounded on an inspection trip, urgently sought a meeting with Hitler. He still wanted to make clear the seriousness of the situation and win his support for an end to hostilities in the West. Why would he have done this if he knew in advance the conspirators' plans to eliminate Hitler?

Misunderstandings

Rommel's problems began with the belief of the men around von Stauffenberg who were planning the resistance that the 'Rommel factor' had to be taken into account in their plans. Even though they considered him Hitler's protégé, they believed he was the embodiment of the soldierly conformist shackled to a morally unscrupulous regime. They calculated that if they could win over Rommel, the most popular soldier in the Reich, then the coup would win wider support among the German people. They also assumed that with Rommel on board it would be easier to open negotiations with the Western Allies for a separate peace or even better to convince them to join with them to oppose the Red Army's drive into Central Europe. Dr Carl Goerdeler, the former Lord Mayor of Leipzig and one of the leading lights of the conspiracy, who was to become Reich Chancellor after Hitler's removal, put Rommel's name on his list, along with several others.

Unbeknownst to Rommel, two officers were to involve him in the coup. One of these was Lieutenant-General Dr Hans Speidel, who had been working in the staff of General Ludwig Beck. In April 1944 Speidel was transferred from the Eastern Front to Rommel's staff at La Roche Guyon. He had recently been decorated with the Knight's Cross and Rommel specifically requested the Chief of Staff from General Otto Wöhler's Eighth Army. With Schmundt's help Rommel was able to get Speidel reassigned. Rommel and Speidel were both from Swabia and had served in the same Stuttgart regiment. Speidel and the Field Marshal differed in one important point, however; Speidel held a PhD in classical philology, and was far superior intellectually and much more crafty.

Speidel had met the military members of the resistance while still in the East. He had been present when Major-General Helmut Stieff and Major-General Henning von Tresckow initiated Wöhler into the plan to remove Hitler. Beck, the head of the military conspiracy, had worked out a plan to arrest Hitler and open the West for the Allies after their expected invasion. Germany could then go on to win the battle against Russia in the East and save Europe from Bolshevism. Speidel entirely agreed with these aims. He was supposed to use the opportunity of his reassignment to the West to try to convince the Field Marshal of the case of the resistance, and if that failed of the need for peace in the West. This assignment was made despite everyone's awareness of the special relationship between Hitler and Rommel. At the end of March the Field Marshal had met with the Wehrmacht Commander of Northern France and Belgium, General Alexander von Falkenhausen. Over dinner von Falkenhausen, who was in constant contact with the conspirators in Berlin, had tried to determine Rommel's attitude toward

An extraordinarily luxurious command post. The chateau of La Roche Guyon on the Seine.

Hitler. He cited Lord Acton's epigram that power corrupts, absolute power corrupts absolutely, to which the Field Marshal made no reply. Falkenhausen felt that he did not get the impression that Rommel 'could be enlisted for action.'[3]

He was supposed to win Rommel over for the resistance and failed: Speidel (right) on the road with his superior.

Consequently Speidel had to proceed cautiously. This caution quickly proved to be necessary as Speidel met with a man who often cursed the aristocratic clique running the Wehrmacht and who had the greatest respect for the Führer. Therefore Speidel's efforts at La Roche Guyon had to be limited primarily to meeting with like-minded men from the headquarters in Paris centred around General Karl-Heinrich von Stülpnagel, the leader of the conspirators in the West. These meetings usually took place when Rommel was away inspecting fortifications and troops on the Atlantic Wall or on the road for days at a time between Brest and the Pas de Calais. Major Eberhard Wolfram, who was on his staff, remembered these times, 'In Rommel's absence Speidel would take the head of the table at meals and the entire conversation revolved around the asshole from the Berghof, a reference to Hitler. When I arrived there was a totally defeatist atmosphere around the company at the table . . . unless Rommel himself was present.'[4]

The conspirators travelled from Paris for another of these evenings on 5 June 1944. 'Der Alte', as they called Rommel, was on leave at home at the time. At the table in the castle was the author Ernst Jünger, who had drafted a peace proclamation, a declaration of a united Christian Europe that was supposed to be ruled by the ideas of human freedom, tolerance and more broadly, particularly social justice. The document also demanded condemnation of those responsible for the war and the mass murders in the concentration camps. It was supposed to be put in mass circulation in Germany and all countries occupied by the Wehrmacht at 'Hour X'.

During the evening at La Roche Guyon, where a large amount was imbibed, the assembled staff ignored radio messages that indicated the Allied invasion was imminent. The Fifteenth Army had picked up a BBC broadcast that contained two lines from a poem by Verlaine, which was known to be a signal for the French Resistance to begin a campaign of sabotage to complement the main operation against the Germans. Shortly after the conspirators had broken up for the evening, at 1:00am on 6 June 1944 Allied airborne landings were being reported from the Conentin peninsula in Normandy. When the information was placed before Speidel, who was responsible for co-ordination of defensive action in the West in Rommel's absence, he hesitated. He assumed that this was just a diversionary tactic and that the main Allied landings would take place farther north at the Pas de Calais as had been predicted for some time. By the time Speidel telephoned the Field Marshal at home in Herrlingen, 100,000 Allied soldiers had already landed and were fighting bitter battles with the surprised and significantly outnumbered German defenders.

D-Day. Rommel was at home in Herrlingen when the invasion began.

Rommel had no indication of the invasion being immi-
nent, and the bad weather apparently reduced the possibility,
an opinion shared by the Supreme Commander West, von
Rundstedt, and the Naval Commander-in-Chief West,
Admiral Theodore Krancke. He had therefore driven home to
celebrate his wife's birthday with her. Then he had planned to
immediately travel on to the Berghof in order to persuade
Hitler to put the reserve Panzer divisions under his command.
What he did not know when he left La Roche Guyon on 4
June for Germany was that the Wehrmacht held undisclosed
information. Since the end of May both the Department for
Foreign Armies West and Himmler's Security Service had a
number of concrete indications that the invasion would be
launched in the next two weeks. The Security Service's

The war in the West must be ended. *Blumentritt, Speidel, Rommel and Rundstedt (from left to right) at La Roche Guyon, June 1944.*

regional headquarters in Paris had reported on 2 June that the preceding day Radio London had broadcast 125 phrases of which 28 were recognised as advance-warning codes. This referred in part to the first line of the Verlaine poem, which meant that the Resistance had received the order to stand by to launch its attacks.

It is not clear whether Speidel ever received this information at La Roche Guyon. What is certain is that Rommel's chief of staff held a completely different view of the defensive battle in the West. While Speidel assumed that the hostilities in France would cease after the removal of Hitler, the Field Marshal was filled with an unrestrained determination to inflict a devastating blow on the Allies. Rommel's great expectations were to be quickly extinguished however; the German Panzer divisions held in the rear could not be thrown into the battle in time. Rommel had believed for too long, a belief reinforced by Speidel, that there would be a second and larger landing at the Pas de Calais.

Although it became apparent soon after the invasion that the battle could no longer be won in the West, Rommel was unwilling to give up hope. During their walks in the park Rommel and his Naval Liaison Officer, Vice Admiral Ruge, agreed 'that we will still be able to survive somehow'.[5] They were betting less on their own forces than on the differences between the Western Allies and the Soviet Union. They believed these were worth taking advantage of so Germany could join with the Western Allies to stem the 'Bolshevik tide' that threatened to break over Europe for the second time since the end of the First World War. The prerequisite for this union was a separate peace in the West – a vain hope since Germany's opponents had long since agreed to demand unconditional surrender.

A view of the 'Atlantic Wall' from the sea. With Ruge (far right) on a patrol boat.

By this time Rommel's opinion coincided with the conspirator Speidel. Both agreed that the massive Allied invasion force could not be halted and that it was time to seek political alternatives. They differed fundamentally, however, on what they understood as 'alternatives'. Speidel, in contrast to Rommel, was clear in that the Western Allies would never make peace with Hitler, so he understood 'alternative' to mean the removal of Hitler, even though he never directly expressed this idea to Rommel. The Field Marshal, on the other hand, was still relying on 'the Führer's political skill' and did not want to believe that he would refuse to take the necessary steps to achieve a separate peace in the West.

Enter Luftwaffe Lieutenant-Colonel Caesar von Hofacker, a cousin of von Stauffenberg and a descendant of Gneisenau, the second officer who was supposed to bring Rommel into the resistance. He had studied law and political science, and as his particular interest was foreign policy, he had been assigned to the military administration in Paris. Hofacker had recognised the criminal nature of Nazism early on and in December 1941 denounced the persecution of the Jews in a letter to his wife: 'Tomorrow another 100 hostages will be shot and 1,500 Jews deported to the East . . . It makes you despair.'[6] He is supposed to have made his decision for a 'system change and the elimination of the Führer' the following year, and is supposed to have discussed this with Goerdeler in January 1944. At the beginning of July 1944 he commented on the planned attempt on Hitler that 'unnecessarily allowing even a few hours to pass [would be] a sin against the Holy Ghost and an offence against my duty as a human being . . .'.[7]

At this point there still was an unsolved problem for those at the centre of the conspiracy in the Parisian headquarters of the Supreme Commander West, where von Hofacker was now a staff officer 'on special assignment': Rommel still had not been won over. Beck had written in June still that 'one could not count on Rommel'. But he was needed if the Western Front was to be 'opened' for the Allies and a path to peace laid there. On 4 August 1944 SS-Obergruppenführer Kaltenbrunner, who was Chief of the Security Police and the Security Service, wrote a report meant for Bormann, 'in place of the German embassy in Paris . . ., von Hofacker was supposed to make all the necessary arrangements to achieve a fundamental agreement with Petain and also to arrange for him becoming the go-between to the English and Americans after the successful assassination.'[8]

General von Stülpnagel sent von Hofacker to La Roche Guyon on 9 July 1944 to win Rommel over to the conspirators' side. Hofacker, who was expected in Berlin by von Stauffenberg on 11 July, made a presentation on the strategic situation to Rommel and his staff. There was more agreement than ever that it was necessary to quickly bring about a political solution to the war in the West to prevent a military collapse. Hofacker most likely did not mention the necessity to eliminate Hitler even in the one-on-one conversation he had with Rommel afterwards; it would have been too obvious. If von Hofacker failed to mention this self-evident truth then it was entirely consistent with the approach of the conspirators. Their method of operation was later analysed by Kaltenbrunner's Security Service using extensive and detailed confessions obtained under torture from those arrested. Kaltenbrunner submitted a report to Bormann on 12 December 1944 that contained the following analysis: only a 'very small circle' was privy to the assassination plot; a 'somewhat wider circle' was to have been informed of the fact 'that a violent undertaking would begin where the question remained open to what extent the Führer would be eliminated; finally the circle of people with which conversations were to be held about the seriousness of the situation, its catastrophic escalation and the necessity for a military state of emergency. A person would only be informed who was immediately involved in the matter and only to the degree necessary'.[9]

Based on the 'need to know' principles of the conspirators, Rommel ought not to have been made privy to the attempt on Hitler – and he surely was not. Even if von Hofacker had spoken about a violent upheaval in Berlin it would not have occurred to Rommel that the elimination of Hitler was implied. His obtuseness was based on the one hand on the political *naiveté* of the simple soldier, on the other by his continuing enthusiasm for National Socialism which had provided him with a great military career.

Rommel was not alone in his attitude toward National Socialism. It was widespread in the officer corps. Fully aware of this, the conspirators of 20 July drafted an appeal to be released after the coup where they referred to themselves as 'soldiers and National Socialists'.[10] They wrote that the army was 'the greatest National Socialist achievement in German history to date.' In a 'life full of work, particularly as soldiers at the front in the [First] World War', they had 'experienced and lived nationalism as selfless duty to the State and social-ism as selfless duty to the nation'. In order to gather the broad-est possible following, the conspirators tried to create the impression that they were the trustees of Hitler's ideals. They were just trying to save them from evil, namely the SS and the party bigwigs, who were seen as those responsible for criminal activities. Rommel had also made this distinction for quite a while, and was still doing so in the summer of 1944. For him Hitler was the personification of National Socialism. For him, therefore, the elimination of the man to whom he had sworn a sacred soldier's oath was therefore unthinkable.

As far as von Hofacker was concerned he had achieved his purpose, because the Field Marshal had immediately declared that he was willing to be involved in making peace with the West in the discussion on 9 July. In the lieutenant-colonel's mind this was decisive: it made Rommel one of the conspirators against Hitler. While Speidel insisted for the rest of his life that there had been no talk about an attempt on Hitler's life during von Hofacker's visit to La Roche Guyon, von Hofacker reported something entirely different on his return to the centre of the conspiracy in Paris. Hofacker is supposed to have enthusiastically told his friend von Falkenhausen, von Stülpnagel and finally his assistant Friedrich Freiherr von Teuchert that he had won Rommel over to the removal of the Führer.[11]

Hofacker met with von Stauffenberg on 11 July as arranged. On the same evening he also reported to General Beck that he had won over Rommel as negotiator with the West. This revelation was by no means met with enthusiasm. Their co-conspirator Hans Berndt Gisevius, who was present at the meeting and had never had anything to do with Rommel, learned on this occasion that Rommel would 'participate' in the *coup*. He testified at the Nuremberg War Crimes Tribunal, 'It would paint a false picture if Field Marshal Rommel now suddenly appeared in the ranks of those who fought against Hitler. Like a typical Party general, Rommel sought to join us [!] very late and we found it distasteful when Herr Rommel, in the face of his personal military disaster, suddenly suggested to us we should have Hitler killed [!], and Göring and

179

Caesar von Hofacker. He claimed to have won Rommel over for the resistance on 9 July 1944.

Himmler too, if possible.'[12] Beck, who could hardly dare to believe the news, is supposed to have attributed the conversion of the otherwise so candid Rommel to 'a complete lack of principle'. They were naturally willing to overlook this character fault since a role was planned for him in ending the war in the West. This must have been what led Beck to the conclusion later in the evening, 'that immediately after the takeover of power important negotiators must be sent to London . . . .'[13] The co-conspirator *Kriegsverwaltungsrat* (an administrator of military rank) Walter Bargatzky was in the meantime working in Paris on the draft of a document that Rommel was supposed to send to Montgomery, his old North African adversary.

The scales only fell from Rommel's eyes about the reason for von Hofacker's visit when he awoke from the coma that resulted from his injuries on 17 July and heard from his *aide-de-camp*, Lang, about the attempt on Hitler's life. The Field Marshal was certainly was not playacting when he voiced his indignation against his fellow officers and is supposed to have turned to Lang and said he now finally understood what von Hofacker had actually been talking about. He later wrote to his wife in the same terms and even talked about meeting Hitler.

On the basis of these accounts neither von Hofacker nor Speidel had won Rommel over for the assassination of their Supreme Commander when von Stauffenberg's explosive device detonated at Führer Headquarters in East Prussia on 20 July. At first it looked as though Hitler had been killed. The Valkyrie Plan, as the putsch was code-named, had started. After long hours of anxious waiting at the conspiracy's Berlin centre, the headquarters of the Reserve Army in the Bendlerstrasse, it failed when it became apparent that the Führer had survived.

While the forces loyal to Hitler in Berlin were soon in control of the situation again, the Paris conspirators still had the reins in their hands, even after it became known that the attempt in faraway Rastenburg had been unsuccessful. Until late in the evening of 20 July the conspirators the Paris conspirators had more than 1,200 SS and SD men, including their leaders, under arrest. While this was going on von Stülpnagel and von Hofacker met with von Kluge. Hofacker urged the Field Marshal to allow the action to continue regardless, but Kluge decided instead to rescind the arrest warrants and relieve the officers of their commands.

In a broadcast on Greater German Radio shortly after midnight Hitler, who had escaped relatively unscathed, announced he would take revenge. This time 'the score [would be] settled in the manner we National Socialists are accustomed to'.[14] As he spoke these words Graf von Stauffenberg, General Friedrich Olbricht, General Beck and others were already dead. Beck had tried to commit suicide, but only seriously injured himself, and was finally shot by a junior officer. The others died before a firing squad in the courtyard of the Army headquarters in Berlin.

A wave of arrests had already begun during the night of 21 July, and it would not take long before it reached the West. Stülpnagel wanted to avoid the impending attentions of the Gestapo by committing suicide. In May he had said to Ernst Jünger: 'leaving life becomes the duty of the competent in certain situations.'[15] Now, in Verdun, von Stülpnagel put a bullet in his head, but only managed to wound himself. Blinded, he was nursed back to health in order to be tortured in the cellars of Gestapo Headquarters in Berlin, dismissed from the Army by its Court of Honour, and finally condemned to death by

Dr Roland Freisler's People's Court. He was led to the gallows in the Plötzensee prison in Berlin on 30 August.

Stülpnagel, Karl Rathgens, a nephew of the same von Kluge who was von Rundstedt's successor as Supreme Commander West, and others had implicated Rommel. Hofacker, the only source for their testimony, had already been condemned to death. The Lieutenant-Colonel, who was staring execution in the face, had explained after his arrest on 25 July that Rommel had shared his opinion that the war was lost and had joined the conspirators. Not only that, but a list containing Rommel's name was found when Goerdeler was arrested. Hitler was made aware of the suspicions surrounding the Field Marshal by Kaltenbrunner's reports, which were forwarded to the Führer Headquarters on 1 August 1944. Hitler was 'shocked' and beside himself. Goebbels, who spent the following day at the Wolfsschanze, wrote in his diary, 'I am being given documents regarding the West conspiracy for 20 July. From these it can be seen that General Stülpnagel was totally involved in this betrayal and that he also tried to pull Kluge and Rommel over to his side. Neither Kluge nor Rommel put up the necessary resistance to his insinuations.'[16] Goebbels was referring indirectly to von Hofacker's attempt to win over Rommel for the resistance, which was traced back to von Stülpnagel's initiative. There was no indication of any active participation by the Field Marshal in the conspiracy, and apparently none was assumed. Nevertheless Hitler, who mistrusted his generals after 20 July, suspected that the conspirators had informed Rommel of the attempt. Goebbels confirmed this in his diary entry of the same day, 'the Führer, too, is convinced that Rommel did not participate in the preparations for the attempt, but that he knew about them. I must say it is . . . the heaviest human disappointment for me. But I have been aware for a long time that Rommel is no "stayer". Politically he has fantastic ideas. He is incredibly useful when things are moving forward, but as soon as a serious crisis appears Rommel is without any inner strength.'[17]

But Hitler's emotional ties to the Field Marshal were too strong for him to call him to account. In addition Rommel did not believe in a 'final victory' anymore and Hitler could not, as the situation on the fronts became more hopeless, put up with being surrounded by officers who had a realistic grasp of the military situation. He had just received such a realistic assessment from Rommel again. Kluge had held back his impassioned plea of 15 July to end the war in the West for several days and as a result it was only presented to Hitler on the 23rd. Rommel's appeal had been strengthened at the end of the month when the Americans made a decisive break-through at Avranches, opening the way to Paris.

Hitler did not view the Field Marshal, whom he had so valued, as a conspirator. As Rommel had 'served his time', the Supreme Commander did not want to play up his possible involvement. Jodl noted, 'Führer lets me read the report, which Kaltenbrunner [Chief of the Security Service] had made concerning the evidence from Lieutenant-Colonel Hofacker. Regarding meeting with R[ommel]. . . . Wants to question R[ommel] after his recovery and then release him without further fuss.'[18]

By the end of August nothing had changed Hitler's mind about the situation. In a meeting which Speidel's successor General Hans Krebs attended, he suggested that Rommel was a great active leader in success, but an absolute pessimist at the 'slightest difficulties'. Warning Krebs never to be on the wrong track, Hitler went on to say that Rommel 'did the worst thing a soldier could do in such a case; he searched for solutions other than military ones'[19] – the solutions the Field Marshal had mentioned several times in his conversations with Hitler.

Rommel had been moved to Herrlingen from a Paris hospital in early August and put under the medical supervision of two Professors of the University of Tübingen, unaware that his name was being mentioned in connection with the conspiracy. He followed the bad news from the Western Front from his sickbed with great concern. When his Chief of Staff unexpectedly visited him on 3 September Rommel not only learned more about the current military situation, but Speidel reported that he had quite suddenly been relieved of his post as Chief of Staff of Army Group B. He told Rommel that the Chief of Staff of the OKW, Field Marshal Keitel, and the Wehrmacht Chief of Staff General Jodl, 'had labelled [Rommel] as a defeatist', and advised him to be careful. 'My husband clearly recognised,' Lucie Rommel later wrote to Speidel in reference to this conversation, 'that a scapegoat for the military events in the West was being sought.'[20]

Rommel, the outsider, knew he had to be careful. He knew he had many enemies in the Wehrmacht because of his meteoric rise, his popularity, and above all Hitler's high regard for him. His enemies had never gotten over the fact that an officer who had not come from the General Staff could rise to the rank of Field Marshal. Back in 1941 Hitler had appointed Rommel to command of the Afrika Korps over the objections of the Army High Command, who had put forward the name of General Hans Freiherr von Funck. Consequently he was resented by both the Supreme Commander of the Army, von Brauchitsch and his Chief of Staff Halder. Rommel's independent methods

185

Competitor for Hitler's favour. Field Marshal Kesselring in conversation with officers of the Afrika Korps.

of operation, which quickly showed itself in the North African campaign and was tolerated by Hitler, caused Halder to angrily write in his diary in April 1941: 'Personal relationships are tarnished as a result of General Rommel's peculiarity and his unhealthy ambition . . . Rommel's character faults allow him to stand out as a particularly unpleasant figure with which no one wishes to get into conflict because of his brutal methods and his support at the highest level.'[21]

His subordinates repeatedly stirred hostility against Rommel. Prime examples were General Streich, whom Rommel had relieved, or the men he had insulted in the heat of battle. One of the latter was Kirchheim, holder of the order Pour-le-Mérite

186

from the First World War. During the battle for Tobruk in April 1941 Rommel had accused him of cowardice and threatened to relieve him over the field telephone. Vice Admiral Eberhard Weichold, the Chief of Naval Command Italy, had frequently clashed with Rommel over questions of supply. He commented disparagingly about Rommel as a 'typical National Socialist *protégé*'. Field Marshal Kesselring, who had been sent to Italy as 'Supreme Commander South' at the end of 1941, had no better relationship with Rommel. Rommel even suspected him of sabotage. Rudolf Rahn, German ambassador in Italy, tried to achieve a rapprochement between the two at a meeting in Fasano on Lake Garda. Rommel said to him, 'Mr. Ambassador, there is no point in trying to mediate between Kesselring and myself, and I want to tell you why. I not only suspect, but actually know, that Field Marshal Kesselring consciously and intentionally delayed the military supply of weapons, munitions and in particular petrol out of jealousy of my fame as a field commander.' When Rahn said that he felt he had to investigate 'the outrageous accusation', Rommel soothingly waved it off and said it was pointless. He knew that Kesselring continued to have 'the ear of the Führer'.[22] Besides, it would be extremely difficult to produce conclusive and legally binding proof in such an investigation. The matter was dropped.

Guderian considered the propaganda show surrounding Rommel as being unworthy of an officer. He had written to his wife in the autumn of 1941, when he was anticipating victory over the Soviet Union and a triumphal entry into Moscow, 'under no circumstances do I want the kind of propaganda à la Rommel made of me'.[[23]] At times Rommel competed with Guderian for the image of the most important 'Panzer General' of the Wehrmacht. They also clashed over how the

Panzer divisions should be deployed in preparation for the Allied invasion of France. Rundstedt also looked down on the '*parvenu*' Rommel, but feared he could oust him from his post as Supreme Commander West. He believed that Rommel was at best a good divisional commander but 'nothing more'.

Rommel's real enemies, however, were all in OKW; in other words, in close proximity to Hitler. For years Jodl and Keitel had to watch Hitler practically idolising his General and later Field Marshal, and inundating him with honours. Jodl later spoke contemptuously of 'Rommel's little shooting expedition in North Africa' at the Nuremberg Tribunal.[24] They believed they had reason to fear that 'Hitler's favourite' would be elevated to Commander-in-Chief of the Army. Their worries were well-founded since Rommel made no secret of his disapproval of the officers of the General Staff. He had made his contempt obvious several times, as for example during the meeting at Führer Headquarters near Soissons in June 1944 in the presence of Keitel and Jodl. He pointed out that no senior officer from around the Führer from OKW had come to the front to see the situation for themselves and the impact of enemy weapons. 'Orders are given from the green table,' according to Rommel, 'judgement of matters from the front are lacking,' and in addition, 'we are expected to trust and they do not trust us themselves'.[25] In his opinion men like Keitel and Jodl were falsely 'influencing' the overtaxed Hitler. Rommel was suggesting that they bore partial responsibility, much in the same way as generals in the First World War, for the confused military situation at the fronts.

The OKW generals took their revenge and tried everything to denigrate him in front of Hitler. Once, when Rommel had drawn Hitler's attention to the seriousness of the situation,

Keitel said to Rommel: 'You have to fight better!' Warlimont, Jodl's deputy, even accused Rommel of cowardice. When Rommel went to Hitler, Warlimont had to apologise to the Field Marshal 'on the orders of the Führer'. Rommel thought he knew that the 'very cold people up there',[26] as he tended to refer to Keitel, Jodl and others, were just waiting for their chance to bring him, 'the awkward Field Marshal', down. He kept this thought in mind during the defensive battle in the West. As a result he kept his most important files, the ones that would exonerate him, close at hand at all times. Ruge recorded another protective measure in his shorthand diary: 'Rommel now always requests permission so the High Command of the Wehrmacht cannot lay blame on him as it always tries.'[27] At another time the Naval Liaison Officer noted that Jodl was trying to 'shoot down' Rommel.[28] When von Rundstedt and one of his Corps commanders were relieved because they reported 'to the top' that the situation at the front was hopeless – as Rommel had before – the Field Marshal thought that he too would be relieved of his post as Supreme Commander of Army Group B. His belief was strengthened after he sent his dramatic appeal via von Kluge on 15 July recommending to Hitler that he end hostilities in the West. Karl Strolin testified on 25 March 1946 as a witness before the Nuremberg Tribunal how Rommel believed his suggestion was 'received' by Hitler. 'Rommel told me after his accident that he fell into disfavour because of this'.[29]

Through all this Rommel still had someone protecting his interests, the Chief of Army Personnel and senior Wehrmacht Adjutant Schmundt, one of Hitler's closest confidantes. For years, the 'ever loyal' Schmundt, whom Rommel called 'Apostle John', had intervened with Hitler on behalf of the 'to be greatly admired Herr Generalfeldmarschall', as he addressed him in numerous letters. He had taken many of Rommel's requests directly to the 'Führer', bypassing Keitel and Jodl, and after Rudolf Hess's flight to England, also bypassing Bormann, Hitler's secretary and head of the Party office. Just before 20 July 1944, when Rommel's relationship with Hitler worsened due to his pessimism about how the war would end, Schmundt had written to the Field Marshal: 'Do not forget that you can always count on me.'[30] But Schmundt would be of no help to the Field Marshal at the decisive moment, as he was critically wounded. Hitler's Chief Adjutant had been standing very close to the bomb that von Stauffenberg had placed under the table in the situation room at the Wolfsschanze.

When Speidel left the Field Marshal in Herrlingen on 5 September 1944 Rommel was even more certain that something was 'brewing' against him. His former Chief of Staff being relieved was a certain indication. When Rommel became aware that Speidel had been arrested by the Gestapo at his home in Freudenstadt the very next day, his fears appeared to have been realised. But Rommel was totally fixated on the military situation. Even then it did not occur to him that Speidel's arrest had any connection to the events of 20 July. So as a comradely gesture to his Swabian countryman he wrote a military justification of Speidel for Hitler's attention. In the letter of 1 October 1944 he wrote that Speidel had already shown himself to be a chief of staff of above average intelligence and efficiency during his first weeks in the West. 'He controlled the staff, showed great sensitivity and loyally helped me to complete the defensive preparations as far as material possibilities allowed. When I was at the front, which occurred most days, I could depend on Speidel executing orders discussed with him previously.' Rommel gave special emphasis to his letter through his closing words, which closely reflected his repeated loyalty vows to Hitler, 'You, my Führer, know that I have always given all my strength and my entire ability, whether during the Western campaign 1940, in Africa 1941–43, in Italy 1943 or again in 1944 in the West. Only one thought ever governed me, to fight and win victory for our new Germany.'[31] It was beyond this innocent's imagination that he would in some way be associated with the assassination attempt. His prejudices against the aristocrats in the officer corps appeared to have been confirmed once again on 20 July, as there were so many of them amongst the conspirators.

The Vicious Circle

When Rommel wrote 'Heil Mein Führer!' at the bottom of that letter on 1 October 1944 Speidel had apparently already heavily implicated him. The tortured von Hofacker had accused the Lieutenant-General of being an accessory to the attempt on Hitler's life. As a way out of his seemingly hopeless situation (the gallows seemed certain), Speidel must have claimed that while von Hofacker had told him the date of the attempt, he had dutifully informed his superior, Rommel. By doing this Speidel passed the responsibility for neglecting to inform the OKW on to Rommel. Whether Speidel's statement was to be believed was supposed to be decided by the Army's Court of Honour), which had to decide whether to dismiss Wehrmacht members from the armed forces and thus turn them over to the jurisdiction of the People's Court.

However, before the Court of Honour could meet the slowly recovering and increasingly depressed Field Marshal had been denounced. When the Kreisleiter of Ulm Maier had visited Rommel in Herrlingen he heard Rommel speak in an excessively defeatist manner. On that occasion Rommel had voiced his total displeasure with the leadership. Hitler was supposed to be surrounded by dilettantes. Incidentally, he had the impression that the 'Führer's mental powers' were deteriorating. This and other statements were received in a roundabout way by one Kronmüller, another Ulm Party member, who believed he could gain advantage for himself by sending a report to Martin Bormann in Berlin.[32]

This was 'grist to the mill' for Bormann, who also had a grudge against Rommel, whom he envied for standing so high in the Führer's favour. When Rommel was commander of the Führer's Headquarters during the Polish campaign he had forbidden Bormann to follow Hitler's car for security reasons and had told him, full of bravado, that this was no 'kindergarten excursion'. He wrote about Rommel, who was now being associated with the resistance, that 'former General Stülpnagel, as well as former Colonel von Hofacker, the already executed nephew of Kluge, Lieutenant-Colonel Rathgens and various still living defendants [have testified] that the Field Marshal was certainly in the picture; Rommel was to have declared that he would be available to the new government after a successful attempt.'[33]

On 27 September, the day that Bormann recorded this in a memorandum, he presented the Kronmüller/Rommel matter to his Führer. In a note that Bormann prepared after his presentation to Hitler he castigated 'the advertising' which Rommel permitted to be created around him. According to Bormann he had 'never [considered Rommel] the military genius that he was being held up to be'. Incidentally people 'who delight in being photographed from morning to night are not the most capable people, because such people would not consider that necessary'. The hate-filled Bormann even commented on Rommel's nearsightedness, as he further wrote that he, 'due to his vanity', he did not even wear spectacles; 'yet he can only read type if he literally holds the paper up to his nose'. In closing he also noted that he had 'dutifully' presented the Kronmüller report to the Führer, 'who discussed its contents with Field Marshal Keitel, R[eichsführer] SS Himmler and General Burgdorf. Further treatment lies in the hands of Field Marshal Keitel.'[34] The same Field Marshal Keitel chaired the Court of Honour a few days later, on 4 October 1944, where Speidel now had to defend himself. In addition to Keitel five other Army generals sat on the Court, including Guderian and Kirchheim. The Chief of the Security Service Kaltenbrunner appeared for the prosecution. Two years after the end of the Second World War Kirchheim and Guderian gave consistent sworn statements on how the Court of Honour session proceeded. They said: 'Kaltenbrunner presented the facts of the case. According to his own explanation Lieutenant-General Speidel learned of the plan for the attempted assassination of 20 July from an officer [referring to von Hofacker] sent by General von Stülpnagel. Whilst he may have reported this to Field Marshal Rommel, since Rommel failed to forward the information it would have been Speidel's duty to promptly report the plan himself. His excuse, that he was not aware that Rommel failed to forward the message, is not credible. Rommel certainly would not have concealed his intent to suppress the message from him in his role as Chief of Staff.'[35]

Kirchheim and Guderian further explained that Kaltenbrunner and Keitel assumed Rommel had been convicted in any event and urged that Speidel be expelled from the Wehrmacht and turned over to the People's Court for sentencing. Keitel and Kaltenbrunner also assumed that Speidel, and in particular Rommel, participated in the attempted subversion. The Court was presented with two choices: it could decide Speidel's testimony was self-serving when he claimed he had dutifully reported the planned attempt to his superior, which would exonerate Rommel; or it could believe Speidel's testimony and thus push sole responsibility onto Rommel. The generals, with Guderian in the lead, chose the second option. Whether they took this course of action because they considered that Rommel was already convicted, or whether they had other reasons, is cloaked in the mists of history. The fact remains that Guderian 'passionately and energetically' tried to make clear to those present that Speidel had fulfilled his duty with his supposed report to Rommel. Keitel responded that Speidel should have confirmed that his superior had reported the matter to Führer Headquarters, at which point Kirchheim retorted that Speidel 'could assume, due to the particularly close relationship of Rommel to the Führer, that Rommel forwarded the message.'[36]

As Kirchheim remembered it, Guderian 'was doubtless primarily responsible for the judges finally arriving at a "not guilty" verdict'. The sequence of events in this session of the Court of Honour was described by Kirchheim to Speidel in a letter from captivity in England in August 1945. Speidel did not contradict Kirchheim's version of the events, rather he confirmed years later that Guderian had 'argued for me in a twenty-minute debate with Keitel'. 'Then he voted for me. So he is thanks to him that a sentencing by the so-called People's Court did not happen.'[37]

Speidel, who later rose to be Commander-in-Chief of NATO Ground Forces in Central Europe, all his life firmly denied the accusation that he had implicated Rommel during his interrogations by the Gestapo. Speidel always answered the question why he was able to survive when Rommel was not by repeating the assertion that von Hofacker had retracted his statement implicating him (Speidel). He wrote in 1945: 'A many-hours long confrontation with the shackled – already condemned – Lieutenant-Colonel Dr. von Hofacker closed the circle of evidence. Dr. von Hofacker was in full command of himself, even though he showed evidence of corporal punishment. In a regal manner, he protected me. In respect of his previous statement about the assassination attempt, he retracted his statement about my being an accessory with the words, "It must have been a memory mix up"'.[38]

Keitel, of all people, supported Speidel's claim after the war, even though he had previously argued for his guilt. The 'Führer's paladin' specifically emphasised during the Nuremberg War Crimes Trial that Speidel had not implicated his former superior, Rommel. He must have been afraid of Speidel, whom he had wanted to send to the gallows, now that the Allies had revived his reputation as a resistance fighter. Keitel did not suspect that Guderian and Kirchheim would give sworn statements in 1947 on that very Court of Honour session, which Keitel had chaired and whose subject had been Speidel's testimony implicating Rommel. At Nuremberg, Keitel spoke of another incriminating moment, which he could not remember anymore (presumably he meant the Goerdeler documents or perhaps the Kronmüller denunciation); he could only remember Lieutenant-Colonel von Hofacker. He was supposed to have testified, according to Keitel, that

Rommel was enthusiastic about the assassination plans which von Hofacker explained to him on 9 July and that Rommel called after him on his departure from La Roche Guyon, 'Tell the gentlemen in Berlin they can count on me when the time comes.'[39] Keitel further claimed that this interrogation transcript, which unequivocally implicated Rommel, was not handed over to the OKW, and then Hitler, until the second week in October. The Lieutenant-Colonel had already been interrogated in July, however, and the interrogation transcripts presented Hitler on 1 August. Apparently Keitel was attempting, for whatever reason, to exonerate Speidel and again distract attention from his joint responsibility for Rommel's fate.

Hitler, whose lenient attitude toward his Field Marshal was slowly eroding, decided to order him to Berlin to clear up the matter once and for all after hearing the Court of Honour's decision. Rommel still believed he would be held responsible for failing to repulse the invasion when the High Command informed Rommel on 7 October that a special train would be sent to Ulm for him on 10 October. He suggested to Ruge, who was visiting him in Herrlingen, that he would not arrive alive. It was not just Rommel's depressed state of mind that contributed to his pessimistic estimate of his situation. In addition, Schmundt, his advocate in Hitler's Headquarters, who had been recovering from his injuries suffered in the explosion at Rastenburg, suddenly died of complications. Luftwaffe Adjutant von Below reported 'that Hitler had not conducted as many confidential conversations with anyone surrounding him as he had with Schmundt',[40] conversations that had continued during Hitler's visits to the patient. Schmundt, who was likely to have tried to convince the Führer that Rommel could not have been involved in the attempt on

Under surveillance by the Gestapo. Rommel's house in Herrlingen.

his life, was no longer alive. The depression-tormented Field Marshal suspected that he had not died of natural causes.

Rommel refused the order to go to Berlin on the grounds that the state of his health did not yet permit such a journey. Unfortunately for Rommel the Gestapo agents had kept his house under close surveillance and reported his advanced state of recovery. To Hitler, this refusal from the otherwise ambitious general was the last piece of circumstantial evidence of his guilt. Shortly thereafter, on 13 October, the telephone rang at the Rommels' house. The OKW announced two officers would visit on the morning of the following day. They were General Wilhelm Burgdorf, Schmundt's successor as Hitler's Chief Adjutant, and General Ernst Maisel, Chief of Matters of Honour in the Army Personnel Office.

The End

When on 14 October the generals showed him the file implicating him in the conspiracy, the Field Marshal was astounded. Just the previous evening he had told his adjutant, Aldinger, 'that the visit is supposed to clarify how we reached the collapse on the Normandy Front'. 'He ordered me to prepare maps so he could present the development of the situation to the generals using sketches.' Rommel's adjutant explained in 1949 at the Munich Denazification Court, 'We were of the opinion that it was supposed to be a kind of justification . . . . The Field Marshal said to me several times "Do you have everything, do you have this or that map?"'[41]

It was only at this moment that Rommel realised what it was all about. He also understood it would be much easier to brand him a traitor than to establish proof of his military failure. Had he not said to von Hofacker and Speidel that necessary political steps would have to be taken after a successful Allied landing in Normandy? Rommel assumed his denunciation was a plot by certain generals. His first question to Burgdorf was whether the Führer knew what was happening. The general's answer made it clear to Rommel that Hitler had been deceived and there would be no reprieve. He had told his wife, Lucie, he would never reach the People's Court, that he would be eliminated before it came to that.

If Rommel did not try to appeal to Hitler, the reason was that he was a broken man in the autumn of 1944. Inevitably, just as in the First World War, it had all been for naught. Certainly, he had risen to Field Marshal. But what about all the sacrifices along the way, particularly those of his troops, who had fallen by the tens of thousands? He had been defeated in North Africa and again in the Allied invasion. The defeat of the Reich was also his own personal defeat. He also recognised that his Supreme Commander no longer had the strength to change the course of destiny as he had done so often in the past eleven years. Rommel believed it was his duty to show loyalty to his Commander-in-Chief, who was staring in the face of the inevitable end like an invalid in his headquarters. Rommel had given up. Not even memories of his great victories could brighten the Field Marshal's mood, not even recalling the storming of Matajur, the victorious dash to the Atlantic with the 7th Panzer Division or the triumphant storming of Tobruk, which had seemed to force open the gate to Egypt. What were these victories in comparison to the catastrophe now confronting the Reich? 'It has grown very dark around us' are the last meaningful words in his book, *War Without Hate*,[42] which he had completed that autumn. He also had dark forebodings for the future. In the summer of 1944 he had said to Admiral Ruge, his partner in walks and conversations in the park at La Roche Guyon, that the most important consideration was the unity of the nation. That was all that needed to be saved.

The closer the end of the war came, the more the Field Marshal's thoughts turned to his own end. He had spoken of death with Ruge, about a soldier's suicide in defeat. 'Repeatedly discussed whether an officer should shoot himself or not.'[43] The dismissed Field Marshal von Kluge, who had also wanted peace with the West, had chosen this path, taking cyanide on 19 August 1944. In a farewell letter to Hitler he had written, 'the [German] nation has suffered so unspeakably that it is time to put an end to this horror.' In an impassioned declaration to Hitler he ended his letter saying, 'I depart this life, my Führer, to whom I was inwardly closer than you might have thought, in the awareness that I have done my duty to the utmost.'[44] Now Rommel was confronted with the painful alternative, to kill himself or be killed. He opted for the former. Burgdorf had outlined for him what Hitler intended if he chose to commit suicide. His honour would be preserved and would not be sullied by unfounded accusations. Hitler assured him he would receive a state funeral and that a monument would be erected in his honour that would commemorate his achievements for 'Führer and Reich'.

And so, at noon on that October day, the Field Marshal entered his final battle, one he knew from the outset he would not win. And yet it still held a purpose for him; it would prevent his wife and son from being persecuted and held liable for his supposed crimes. Lucie Rommel reported her husband's dramatic farewell: 'I find it impossible to express what could be read in his face. In answer to the question what was the matter, my husband answered absentmindedly, "I will be dead in a quarter of an hour".

On Hitler's instructions he was given the choice to allow himself to be poisoned or to be put in front of the People's Court.' In response to the question why, he answered he was being accused of participation in the 20 July affair. General von Stülpnagel, Lieutenant-General Speidel and Lieutenant-Colonel von Hofacker had made statements implicating him. Beyond that he was apparently designated Reich President on Goerdeler's list. 'My husband answered the Generals Burgdorf and Meisel [*sic*!] that he did not believe that because it was all a fabrication,' it could at best be the result of 'known methods of blackmail'.[45]

Rommel then said farewell to his 15-year-old son and to his adjutant, Aldinger, who had served with him in the Württemburg Mountain Regiment. To the latter he said, 'I had no part in the assassination attempt. I have served my Fatherland my entire life and done my best. Give my regards to my Swabian people and in particular to my beloved old Mountaineers.'[46] In full uniform, and with his Field Marshal's baton in hand, Rommel finally left the house. 'We accompanied him as far as the vehicle,' his son later wrote, 'where the generals greeted him with "Heil Hitler". My father was the first to climb in and took a seat in the rear. Then the vehicle drove off in the direction of Blaubeuren.'[47]

An SS corporal named Heinrich Doose, the vehicle driver, described what happened next. Two hundred metres beyond the Herrlingen town limits General Burgdorf told him to stop. 'General Maisel took me away, a little further up the road. After a little time, about five to ten minutes, Burgdorf called us back to the vehicle. I saw Rommel sitting in the back of the car, obviously dying, unconscious, collapsed into himself, sobbing, not moaning or groaning, but sobbing. His cap had fallen off. I sat him upright and put his cap back on his head.'[48] The intrepid

He brought Rommel the potassium cyanide capsule. Burgdorf, Schmundt's successor as Hitler's Adjutant.

troop leader of two World Wars had bitten on the poison capsule that Keitel had sent him. Then it became quiet in the rear of the little Opel. Field Marshal Erwin Rommel was dead.

As previously arranged, Generals Burgdorf and Maisel immediately took Rommel's body to a reserve hospital in Ulm. Once there two medical orderlies carried him to an operating theatre. An unsuspecting medical captain was told the Field Marshal had suffered a heart attack. After futile resuscitation attempts an SS man appeared and requested a private conversation with the duty medic, but he refused to sign Rommel's death certificate with the diagnosis 'heart attack, resulting from accident in line of duty in the West'.[49] This was eventually taken care of by another physician, who also specified the Field Marshal's body was to be cremated. Shortly thereafter Lucie Rommel was notified. Her husband was supposed to have been taken ill suddenly and admitted to hospital, 'apparently the result of an embolism'. All medical help, however, came too late. At the same time a 'leadership special priority telephone call' was made from the Ulm city headquarters. General Burgdorf reported to Keitel 'mission accomplished'.

It was reported to Hitler very briefly in the evening situation review that Rommel had died as a result of a motor vehicle accident during the Western campaign. His only reaction was an expressionless 'another one of the old ones'.[50] After the recent loss of Schmundt, to Hitler the suicide by poison of his Field Marshal appeared as evidence that the latter had turned against him. He was unwilling to admit such a personal defeat publicly, so he tried to maintain the fiction of Rommel's embolism even to his immediate circle. The entire Führer Headquarters was having difficulty with the 'true reasons' for the Field Marshal's supposed participation in the resistance, rumours of which were becoming increasingly pervasive. Hitler's Luftwaffe Adjutant, von Below, wrote in his memoirs: 'We were all in agreement that Rommel could only have been turned against Hitler by the influence of third parties, hardly of his own accord.'[51] And Alfred-Ingemar Berndt, Rommel's confidant and link to the top echelons of the Reich for many years, wrote to Lucie Rommel in October 1944, before he fell in Hungary, that the Reichsführer-SS was not a party to her husband's death. 'He is most deeply shattered.' Hitler was said to also have been deceived. 'All this is the work of Keitel and Jodl.'[52]

Hitler kept his promise to protect Rommel's reputation. In his Order of the Day on the Field Marshal's death it was then reported he had succumbed to complications from the serious injuries he had suffered in a motor vehicle accident during a tour of the Front as Supreme Commander of an Army Group.

Pompous production at Hitler's instructions. The state funeral in Ulm.

In Rommel the Army had lost one of its best leaders. 'In the current fateful battle his name represents outstanding bravery and fearless daring for the German nation. . . . The Army lowers the Reich War Flag in proud sorrow for this great soldier.'[53]

Hitler arranged a funeral service, which was shown in newsreels in those cinemas still standing in the Reich. It would have lived up to the Field Marshal's reputation had it not been so hypocritical. All available troops in the Ulm area were mustered. Four honour companies fell-in in front of the City Hall of the Swabian town. A military band played funeral marches continuously, making the attendees shudder. Amongst those affected were probably some of the many high-ranking officers who had assembled there. Generals of the Army kept the guard of honour at the coffin, which enshrouded by a huge swastika flag. On it lay Rommel's steel helmet and marshal's baton. In front, on a velvet pillow, rested his decora-

204

tions: most prominently displayed were his Pour-le-Mérite and the Knight's Cross of the Iron Cross with Oak Leaves and Swords and Diamonds. When the dead Field Marshal's family members entered the hall the Funeral March from Wagner's *Götterdämmerung* rang out.

The eulogy, prepared by the Propaganda Ministry for the OKW, was delivered by Field Marshal von Rundstedt 'in the name of the Führer who as the Supreme Commander has called us to this place to take our leave from his Field Marshal who has been left on the field of honour. . . . The German nation has loved and celebrated Field Marshal Rommel in a truly unique manner.' With him 'such a great soldierly leader has gone from us as is only rarely given to a nation. Deeply rooted in German soldierdom he dedicated his life exclusively to work and the struggle of Führer and Reich.' He was 'imbued' with 'the spirit of National Socialism'. This spirit gave him his strength and was the motivating force of his actions. Rundstedt closed with the words 'his heart belonged to the Führer'[54] and laid down Hitler's huge wreath, just before the cynical and at the same time so truthful '*Ich hatt' einen Kameraden*' ('*I had a comrade*') was played.

Lucie and Manfred Rommel had maintained appearances and tolerated the hypocritical production to the bitter end for the sake of the dead Field Marshal. In the preceding days they had received letters of condolence by the sackful. In addition to the letter from Goebbels and his wife, which expressed their 'deepest sympathy', was a telegram from the Führer. It read, 'Please accept my sincere condolences on the heavy loss you have suffered as a result of your husband's death. The name of Field Marshal Rommel will be forever linked to the heroic battles in North Africa. Adolf Hitler.'[55]

GENERAL FELDMA
ERWIN R

5

The Legend

The mysterious death of Field Marshal Erwin Rommel led to widespread speculation in Germany shortly after the end of the war. It was questioned whether the Field Marshal actually died of complications from his serious injuries as Nazi propaganda had claimed. Rommel's son ended the speculation with a sworn statement made on 5 April 1945, which was published in the first postwar edition of the *Südkurier* on 8 September 1945, in which he said that the Field Marshal did not die of natural causes, but was eliminated on the orders of Hitler. In an exact account of the events of 14 October 1944 Manfred Rommel wrote that his father had said, as he was making his last good-bye, 'he had been suspected of participating in the 20.07.1944. His former chief of general staff, Lieutenant-General Speidel, who had been arrested a few weeks earlier, was supposed to have testified that my father participated in 20.07.1944 in a leading capacity and was only prevented from taking part directly as a result of being wounded. General Stülpnagel had made the same statements. . . . In addition, my father appeared as Ministerpräsident on Lord Mayor Goerdeler's list. The Führer did not want to debase his memory in the eyes of the German nation and gave him the option of suicide by poison capsule.'[1]

This revealing explanation by Manfred Rommel was followed only a few weeks later in the *Südkurier* of 16 October by two further statements.[2] One was by Hans Speidel, who had survived the war. After the Court of Honour proceedings he was initially confined at the fortress of Küstrin. Later he was taken to the Hersberg Monastery near Immenstadt in the Allgäu, where he was eventually liberated by French troops under General Bathouard. In his statement Speidel contradicted the account presented by Manfred Rommel. Speidel wrote: 'I never made such a statement, not even in spirit, in front of the Gestapo; to the contrary, I described participation by the Field Marshal in 20.07.1944 as totally groundless. Moreover, such a statement would have only implicated me.' The latter was believable because if Speidel had testified that Rommel was a 'leading participant in 20.07.1944' he would not have been able to save himself from the Gestapo with the argument that he had, after hearing of the plot, reported it to his superior, Rommel.

Lucie Rommel obviously took this argument into account when she wrote the second explanation printed in the 16 October 1945 edition of the *Südkurier*. She understood her son's statement, and its implied blame on Speidel, differently. She wrote that her husband was told by Hitler's messengers that 'General von Stülpnagel, Lieutenant General Dr. Speidel and Lieutenant-Colonel von Hofacker had made implicating statements. My husband answered the Generals Burgdorf and Meisel [*sic!*] that he did not believe it because it was a fabrication'.[3]

Of course the conjectures surrounding Rommel's possible entanglement in the assassination attempt on Hitler did not end with these explanations. Instead they added more fuel to the fire. This was easy to understand, as why else would Rommel been forced to his death? The Field Marshal's widow was concerned to preserve her late husband's reputation and wrote to an acquaintance. She wanted his help 'to correct the many publications in radio and press and the equally numerous rumours in order to keep the name Rommel pure and preserve the honour of Field Marshal, a son of Württemburg'. 'I would like to once again establish that my husband did not participate in the preparations and execution of 20.07.1944 because as a soldier he rejected taking such a path. My husband had forever honestly represented his opinions, his intentions and his plans to the highest levels, . . . even when these higher levels and the leadership did not find this comfortable. During his entire career he was always a soldier and never a politician . . .'.[4]

The widow of the Field Marshal kept careful watch that nothing should damage his reputation (by associating him with the plot), because the dominant feeling in early postwar Germany was to want to have nothing to do with the conspiracy. In the eyes of most people the conspirators were traitors and outcasts. The Germans had not grasped neither the reality nor the scale of the genocide of the Jews, or the other crimes committed in their name, and to an extent had no desire to comprehend that reality. They felt they shared a common destiny. They had been defeated, and the guilt and responsibility had been applied to them collectively by the victors. Support for the resistance was also repressed because millions of Germans had also suffered dreadful injustice as a result of the bombing, expulsion and deportation. The journalist Eugen Kogon, himself a survivor of the Buchenwald concentration camp, wrote in 1949 that the defeated nation was shown with the end of the war, 'that Hitler's spirit lives on in others, not just in Germans, because the world's susceptibility to totalitarian methods has become apparent; . . . because the horror that is in the past loses its impact among the confused horrors that are present.'[5] In his remarks Kogon had in mind the new dictatorship that was being created in the Soviet Occupation Zone. Given the new reality of the Cold War, the Western Allies' new view of the communist enemy began to coincide with the Germans' old conception of the Bolshevik enemy, just as Nazi propaganda had pounded it into them. The Western Allies were laying the groundwork for establishing a democratic West German state with a concomitant defence requirement. They therefore declared the Wehrmacht an honourable opponent despite its involvement in Hitler's racially-motivated war of extermination. The initial moral ostracism of his accomplices came to a rapid end after the 'Iron Curtain' had descended over Europe.

Hans Speidel, Rommel's Chief of Staff in the West, was one of the very first generals of the Wehrmacht to recognise the new signs of the times. As a resistance fighter against Hitler he possessed a certain standing with the victors in the new political reality, which he quickly understood how to use. He wrote memoranda promoting German rearmament. As a prerequisite for this he identified a 'true peace'. Justice must encompass all people, 'even the defeated soldiers and the millions of fallen,' he wrote, referring to the philosophy of Karl Jaspers. 'The conscience of soldierly honour remains unaffected by all discussions of blame. He who was loyal in comradeship, unwavering in danger, proven by courage and objectivity, may guard something unimpeachable in his self-awareness', Jaspers wrote.[6]

Faithful to this guiding principle Speidel successfully fought for the rehabilitation of the German Wehrmacht and its military leadership, most of whom were sitting in prison like Manstein. He carefully planned a very special role for one leader in particular – Field Marshal Rommel, who, with such

212

He intended to make Rommel a 'national hero'. Speidel with Lucie Rommel, October 1959.

a reputation, even with the enemy, was to become the symbol of a better German military tradition. Speidel announced his intention when he met with Panzer General Leo Freiherr Geyr von Schweppenburg, one of a small team of Wehrmacht officers writing an account of the invasion battle for the Americans. As von Schweppenburg remembered it, and also recounted in a sworn statement, Speidel told him during a three-day meeting that he 'intended to make Rommel a national hero of the German people'.[7] In order to be a role model in a democratic society of the future Rommel had to have belonged to the resistance against Hitler. Subsequently Speidel was the instigator of an article which was printed in the newspaper *Christ und Welt* in September 1948, honouring Rommel as a soldier, and also provided 'details' for the first time of his resistance activities. Rommel's remarks about Hitler 'were at their sharpest' in the weeks before the Allied landings in Normandy. And it further said that 'meetings took place with the military leader in France, von Stülpnagel, who was later executed, about the preparations for cease-fire negotiations with Eisenhower and Montgomery without reference to Hitler. . . . Rommel clung to the thought of arresting Hitler, possibly using reliable Panzer units. He did not want to create a martyr; he preferred that Hitler be condemned by a German court.'[8] The article announced a forthcoming book in which Speidel was to explore Rommel's role in the resistance in greater detail. The book came out at the end of 1949 under the title *Invasion 1944: a Contribution to the Fate of Rommel and the Reich*. In it Speidel transformed Rommel into one of the leaders of the resistance, 'Rommel's realisation and decision came late. His conscience as a soldier only slowly expanded to the political and tried to advance into the religious: with the fruit of Jünger's ideas of peace, which allowed him a glimpse of virgin territory, into the mysterious interrelationship of belief and reality. Fate intervened when he was ready to step into action.'[9] Ernst Jünger emphasised this fate dramatically in his introduction to *Radiations* when he wrote that the shot that hit Rommel on 17 July 1944 on the road to Livarot robbed 'the plot of the only shoulders to which the dreadful double weight of war and civil war could be entrusted, the only man who possessed sufficient naïveté to oppose the dreadful simplicity of those to be attacked. It was an unambiguous omen.'[10]

Speidel's early legend of the resistance fighter was established in the first Rommel biography, which appeared in 1950. Its author was the British General Desmond Young. He presented Rommel's supposed participation in the conspiracy against Hitler, but also gave an answer to the question why Speidel was able to survive. According to him, von Hofacker had retracted his statement that implicated Speidel. The rest was a 'spiritual exercise in dialectics' according to Young and cited Rommel's Chief of General Staff's words, 'I believe it was because I remained totally calm and without any emotional outburst, acting according the methods of logic. I suggested to them that I was not concerned about my own fate.' Young went on to conclude that Speidel almost succeeded in convincing the Gestapo that it would have been totally impossible that Rommel 'had even the slightest bit to do with the events of 20 July.'[11]

As far as Rommel's role as an army commander was concerned, Young's book became a posthumous tribute by the victors to the vanquished. It was forcefully expressed in the introduction, contributed by no less a person than the Supreme Commander of the British Middle East forces, by then Field Marshal Sir Claude Auchinleck. Honouring Rommel's leadership in North Africa was made easier because it was not the scene of Hitler's racially-motivated war of annihilation, of millions of deaths and the absolute misery of the civilian population. The huge killing machinery of the Holocaust was also absent. The well-known British historian Sir Basil Liddell-Hart also treated the subject of Rommel in an exceedingly fair manner early on. Two years after Young's book he published the German Field Marshal's notes on the Western campaign, the African campaign and the defence of Normandy together with Rommel's letters under the title *The Rommel Papers*.

It is obvious why the British in particular should devote so much attention to a Field Marshal of the still-hated Germans (it is remarkable to note that the first five Rommel biographies were written by Englishmen). By the fall of 1942 the British had been driven out of continental Europe; North Africa was the only remaining ground theatre of war where they opposed the Wehrmacht. The longer the war dragged on the more Great Britain's political and military importance in the Anglo-American-Soviet coalition waned. In order to present their own participation in the defeat of Germany in the best possible light they had to build up the importance of the war in North Africa. Accordingly the army commanders deployed there were celebrated by the British, particularly Montgomery, who was raised to the peerage as 'Viscount Montgomery of Alamein' for his victory over the significantly-inferior German Panzerarmee in November 1942. Rommel had been portrayed as a 'superman' in British propaganda in order to minimise their reverses in North Africa in 1941/42. After the war he retained the image of an exceptional field commander; if he was already impressive, how much more impressive was the man who eventually defeated him?

The victors restored the reputation of the German soldier, indeed of Germany as a whole, with the myth of Rommel. From the perspective of the Western Allies this was unavoidable because German soldiers of the newly-founded Bundeswehr were to serve alongside them. Thus Speidel's plan practically executed itself, not least for him personally. Rommel's former Chief of Staff, who had initially become Adenauer's Chief Military Adviser, joined the *Amt Blank*[12] in 1951 and later served as Germany's chief delegate in the negotiations for the German contribution to a European Defence Union. In December 1955 he was officially reactivated as Lieutenant-General of the Bundeswehr and was officially posted as Chief of the 'Armed Forces Department' in the Bonn Ministry of Defence. Later he succeeded Montgomery and the French Generals Jean de Lattre de Tassigny and Marcel-Maurice

216

Time heals all wounds. Lucie Rommel and Speidel in the Herrlingen cemetery in the 1960s

Carpentier as Supreme Commander of NATO Ground Forces Central Europe in April 1957.

Meanwhile, Rommel became a legend as the 'Desert Fox'. A flood of publications created this image. In 1950 alone two other works appeared in wide circulation alongside Young's biography, which had become a bestseller in Germany. The Field Marshal's widow, in co-operation with his former Divisional Chief of Staff Fritz Bayerlein, published Rommel's notes of the three theatres of war, and his former war correspondent, von Esebeck, brought out a history of the Afrika Korps under the title *African Years of Destiny.* But that is not all. Rommel had long since returned to the cinema screen, portrayed by American actors. After *Five Graves to Cairo* had been filmed in 1946 a second film followed in 1951 that closely mirrored the literature being published on the Field Marshal. Even if it was titled *The Desert Fox*, not *Victory in Africa,* the title Rommel had prophesied to the Italian officers shortly after his arrival in Tripoli in 1941, it was still something of a belated victory. Its premiere in Stuttgart was attended by relatives of the Field Marshal and former generals of the Afrika Korps as well as by Speidel, even though he was unpopular among the 'Afrikaners'.

And so the picture that most people had formed of the African theatre of war and more particularly of the German Field Marshal was reinforced. The Allied press, as well as Goebbels' propaganda, had originally painted the portrait; now it was being repeated without the Nazi pathos. A distorted image emerged which featured a contest between great field commanders. Rommel was compared to Hannibal and Napoleon; strategists of no lesser stature were chosen for Montgomery. In the expanses of North Africa they showed 'desert foxes' against 'desert rats' in a chivalrous battle. The tenor of the image was captured in the emotive words inscribed on a memorial erected a few kilometres from the site of the battle of El Alamein to honour the fallen German troops: 'Whether friend or foe or brother, whether sons of Germany, Italy or England – your conduct was chivalrous, your law was humane here.'

The old Africa campaigners were able to organise early on without being looked at critically by the Allied Occupation Forces who would soon become allies and friends. In 1950 the field newspaper, *Die Oase*, founded during the war, reappeared for the first time. Now it was published by the 'Verband Deutsches Afrika Korps e. V.' and the 'Rommel Sozialwerk e. V.'. The 'Afrikaners', as the veterans were known, began to assemble again at reunions in many towns throughout the Federal Republic and Austria. The last surviving veterans of the

218

Colonial Army who had served in the former colony of German East Africa had their get-togethers at those same reunions of the 1950s. The high point of these affairs was the annual national meeting. Out in front was their former commander, the aged and venerable von Lettow-Vorbeck, in khaki uniform and pith helmet and wearing the Pour-le-Mérite, just as Rommel had done. They exchanged memories of long ago or made plans to journey to the distant graves of old comrades before they sang. But they did not sing the songs of the Afrika Korps, of the Panzers sweeping toward Egypt; instead they sang the song of the old German colonial army of the First World War. 'How often did we march on the narrow Negro path, through the middle of the plains, when the early morning is dawning; how we listened to the sounds of the familiar songs of the bearers and Askari, Heia, Heia Safari . . .'.

The Bundeswehr soon sent delegations to these reunions and also to the annual memorial ceremony at the Herrlingen cemetery on the anniversary of Rommel's death. After all, the Field Marshal was a role model for the armed forces of democratic Germany. In November 1961 a commemorative plaque was unveiled in Goslar, where Rommel had served as a battalion commander for eighteen months. The Inspector General of the Bundeswehr, General Friedrich Foertsch, made an appearance and honoured Rommel 'as the most magnificent soldier and great man', who will always be 'a role model and obligation for us young soldiers'.[13] The dedication speech in Goslar was delivered by General Hoth, who had been sentenced to 15 years imprisonment at Nuremberg, but then released early when the political climate changed. Hoth spoke of the honour of the German soldier personified in Rommel, but not of his putative participation in the resistance.

The image of Rommel, the belated resistance fighter, whose name appeared on barracks and a Bundeswehr destroyer, contributed to the fact that the legend of the 'Desert Fox' lasted into the 1960s. Only then, with a new generation, did critical discussion of the Nazi past begin. The burden of inheritance of the Hitler dictatorship entered the consciousness of the West Germans after the Adolf Eichmann and Auschwitz trials. The question of guilt was now posed; the role of the elite, of industry, and in particular of the Wehrmacht, in Hitler's racially-motivated war of annihilation was critically examined. In the face of this potentially soul-destroying self-examination the resistance to Hitler, which included a small group of mostly aristocratic officers, was seen in a totally different light. The conspiracy of the men of 20 July 1944, which had been part and parcel of the Federal Republic's legitimisation, was now recognised and honoured by the majority of the population as a moral act that symbolised a better Germany. This ended the debate that the officer corps had long held about the value of the soldier's oath.

The time had also come for Rommel's widow to end her resolute defence of her husband's honour against allegations that he had been one of the conspirators of 20 July, and Manfred Rommel adjusted his declaration of April 1945, which had been forgotten. In November 1974 he wrote in response to an enquiry from the revisionist historian David Irving that he had been 16 years old at the time. His father did 'not doubt for one second' Speidel's loyalty. As he knew from him, 'he had at no point in time admitted anything about his or my father's participation in the planned attempt on Hitler.'[14] The above-mentioned historian, who denies Hitler's authorship of the Holocaust, published a wide-ranging biography of

Rommel in 1977. For the first time, this book presented Rommel as a follower of the 'Führer' who remained loyal to his soldier's oath to Hitler to the last. There is no doubt that Irving's interpretation of Rommel's relationship to the resistance represents a change in historical viewpoint. Later treatments of the Field Marshal, for example those by Dieter Ose[15] and David Fraser,[16] follow his interpretation in that particular respect.

If the image of Rommel eventually changed during the last two decades of the twentieth century it can be attributed to, among other things, the fact that the manner in which the Germans dealt with their history had evolved even further. At the beginning of the 1980s historians argued whether the Nazi crimes were unique. In the 1990s Germans again discussed the question of the collective guilt of the postwar period. Increasingly politics and self-flagellation, not thinking of the Third Reich in historical terms, determined the discourse from then on in a society with an ever-increasing lack of historical awareness, which seems to measure the past exclusively with the values and moral standards of the present. Rommel was now quickly converted into a 'war criminal', as the journalist Ralph Giordano did in his book, *The Falsehood of Tradition*.[17] The demand to rename the Bundeswehr barracks that carry his name is a recurring ritual in politics. The memorial plaque was removed from the former officer's mess of the Goslar battalion in May 2001, using the same argument that Rommel was representative of a criminal regime.

After a Rommel documentary in the ZDF (Second German Television) under the overall control of Guido Knopp[18] the filmmaker Maurice Remy produced a TV documentary *cum* book in 2002. The latter marked another turning point when the legend of the Field Marshal as Speidel had created it after

221

A wooden cross in the Herrlingen cemetery serves as a reminder of probably the best-known German soldier of the Second World War.

the war returned in Remy's *The Rommel Myth*. Rommel became the 'hero of the resistance', although with the qualification that he had also been a 'convinced National Socialist' for a very long time. 'Rommel was both,' Remy concludes.

In reality Rommel was neither the one nor the other. He had intrinsically understood neither National Socialism, nor the resistance to it. In this respect Rommel epitomises millions of Germans. The German tragedy is reflected in the persona of the Field Marshal as a prototype. He followed the Führer, who had restored the self-esteem of a humiliated nation, into disaster and whilst doing so believed he was only doing his duty.

Endnotes

Chapter 1

1 Erwin Rommel, *Infanterie greift an. Erlebnis und Erfahrung* (Potsdam: 1941) p 8.
2 Adolf Hitler, *Mein Kampf* (Munich: 1939) p 167.
3 Hitler, *Kampf*, p 167.
4 Hitler, *Kampf*, p 168
5 Ralf Georg Reuth, *Hitler. Eine politische Biographie* (Munich: 2003) p 34.
6 'Rommel's Personnel File 1910–1944' in EP Microform Limited (ed), *Selected Documents on the Life and Campaigns of Field Marshal Erwin Rommel* (East Ardsley, Wakefield) Roll 1, hereafter *SDLC*.
7 Rommel, *Infanterie*, p 82f.
8 Rommel, *Infanterie*, p 341.
9 Rommel, *Infanterie*, p 340.
10 Kurt Hesse, 'Wandlung eines Mannes und eines Typus', Typewritten Manuscript, 1945, in *SDLC*, Roll 3.
11 Reuth, *Hitler*, p 457.
12 Reuth, *Hitler*, p 48.
13 Hitler, *Kampf*, p 205.
14 Joachim C Fest, *Hitler. Eine Biographie* (Frankfurt aM/Berlin/ Vienna: 1973) p 105.
15 Desmond Young, *Rommel der Wüstenfuchs*, with an introduction by Sir Claude Auchinleck (Wiesbaden: 1974) p 268.
16 Rommel, *Infanterie*, p 400.
17 Bodo Scheurig, *Alfred Jodl – Gehorsam und Verhängnis* (Berlin/Frankfurt aM: 1991) p 21.
18 *Völkischer Beobachter*, 4 February 1933.

19 Oswald Spengler, *Jahre der Entscheidung* (Munich: 1933) p VIII.

20 Young, *Rommel*, p 53.

21 David Irving, *Rommel. Eine Biographie* (Hamburg: 1978) p 37.

22 Letter to Lucie Rommel, 24 November 1939, National Archives (herafter NA), RG 242 T 84/273.

23 *Der Prozess gegen die Hauptkriegsverbrecher vor dem Internationalen Militärgerichtshof, Nürnberg 1948* (Nürnberg: 1948) Vol XXV, Doc 386-PS, p 1161 ff, hereafter *IMT*.

24 Young, *Rommel*, p 88.

25 Reuth, *Hitler*, p 574.

26 Letter to Lucie Rommel, 2 December 1938, NA RG 242 T 84/272.

27 Nikolaus von Below, *Als Hitlers Adjutant 1937-45* (Mainz: 1980) p 239.

28 Hesse, 'Wandlung', Roll 3.

29 Letter to Lucie Rommel, 2 September 1939, NA RG 242 T 84/273.

30 Young, *Rommel*, p 60f.

31 Letter to Lucie Rommel, 9 November 1939, NA RG 242 T 84/273.

32 Young, *Rommel*, p 65.

33 Letter to Lucie Rommel, 19 September 1939, NA RG 242 T 84/273.

34 Letter to Lucie Rommel, 10 September 1939, NA RG 242 T 84/273.

35 Irving, *Rommel*, p 52.

36 Walter Warlimont, *Im Hauptquartier der deutschen Wehrmacht 39-45* (Munich: 1978) p 52.

37 Letter to Lucie Rommel, 22 October 1939, NA RG 242 T 84/273.

38 *IMT*, Vol XXIX Doc 1992-PS A, p 234.

39 'Befragung Manfred Rommels durch David Irving am 5 December 1976', in *SDLC*, Roll 3.

40 Ralf Georg Reuth, *Rommel – Des Führers General* (Munich: 1987) p 31.

41 Letter to Lucie Rommel, 17 February 1940, NA RG 242 T 84/273.

42 Letter to Lucie Rommel, 13 April 1940, NA RG 242 T 84/273.

43 Young, *Rommel*, p 89.

44 Young, *Rommel*, p 89.

45 Letter to Lucie Rommel, 26 December 1940, NA RG 242 T
   84/273. Rommel repeated the contents of Schmundt's and
   Hitler's letters in this letter.
46 Letter to Lucie Rommel, 26 December 1940, NA RG 242 T
   84/273.
47 Reuth, *Rommel*, p 34.
48 *Akten zur Deutschen Auswärtigen Politik, Series D. 1937 to 1945*
   (Baden-Baden: 1950ff) Vol XII.i, Doc 17, 5.2.1941, p 25.
49 Schmundt to Rommel, 19 February 1941, NA RG 242 T 84/276.
50 Schmundt to Rommel, 19 February 1941, NA RG 242 T 84/276.
51 Below, *Adjutant*, p 264.
52 Hitler to Rommel, 1 January 1942, Bundesarchiv-Militärarchiv
   Freiburg (hereafter BA-MA), N 117/3.
53 Walter K Nehring, 'Begleitwort' in Charles B Burdick,
   Unternehmen Sonnenblume. Der Entschluss zum Afrika-Feldzug
   (Neckargmünd: 1972) p 9.
54 Irving, *Rommel*, p 203.
55 Irving, *Rommel*, p 203.
56 Letter to Lucie Rommel, 7 July 1941, NA RG 242 T 84/274.
57 Letter to Lucie Rommel, 23 June 1941, NA RG 242 T 84/274.
58 Henry Picker, *Hitlers Tischgespräche im Führerhauptquartier*
   (Frankfurt/Berlin: 1989) 9 September 1942, p 433.
59 Elke Fröhlich (ed), *Die Tagebücher des Joseph Goebbels*, commissioned
   by the Institut für Zeitgeschichte and with support from the
   Staatliche Archivdienst Russlands (Munich 1987–2001) 26 volumes, II 4, 1 October 1942, p 38, (hereafter Fröhlich, *Goebbels*).
   Hereafter, where the citation is also in the Piper-Auswahl-Edition
   edited by the author, it will be shown in parentheses: Ralf Georg
   Reuth (ed), *Goebbels, Joseph: Tagebücher 1924-1945*, Vols 1–5
   (Munich: 2000), hereafter Reuth, *Goebbels*.
60 Irving, *Rommel*, p 406.
61 Vice Admiral Friedrich Ruge, 'Stenographic Diaries from
   December 1943 – October 1944', 25 June 1944, in *SDLC*, Roll 2.
62 Percy Ernst Schramm (ed), *Kriegstagebuch des Oberkommandos der
   Wehrmacht (Wehrmachtführungsstab)* Vol I–IV (Munich: 1982) Vol
   II, 3 November 1942, p 895, note 2.
63 Hitler's radio message, 3 November 1942, BA-MA, RH 19 VIII/26.
64 Copy of OKW radio message to Rommel, 4 November 1942, NA
   RG 242 T 84/276.

65 Friedrich Ruge, *Rommel und die Invasion, Erinnerungen* (Stuttgart: 1959) p 230.

66 Heinz Linge, *Bis zum Untergang. Als Chef des persönlichen Dienstes bei Hitler* (Munich: 1980) p 21.

67 Warlimont, *Hauptquartier*, Fragment Nr. 8, 12 December 1942, p 316.

68 Warlimont, *Hauptquartier*, Fragment Nr. 8, 12 December 1942, p 316.

69 Warlimont, *Hauptquartier*, Fragment Nr. 8, 12 December 1942, p 317.

70 Fröhlich, *Goebbels*, Vol II. 7, 14 January 1943, p 111f (Reuth, *Goebbels*, Vol 5, p 1870f).

71 Letter from Berndt to Lucie Rommel, 8 February 1943, in *SDLC*, Roll 11.

72 Fröhlich, *Goebbels*, Vol II.7, 12 March 1943, p 535.

73 Fröhlich, *Goebbels*, Vol II.8, 11 May 1943, p 274.

74 Fröhlich, *Goebbels*, Vol II.8, 10 May 1943, p 266.

75 Reuth, *Rommel*, p 45f.

76 Warlimont, *Hauptquartier*, Fragment Nr 46, 31 August 1944, p 482.

77 Letter to Lucie Rommel, 9 November 1943, NA RG 242 T 84/275.

78 Irving, *Rommel*, p 432.

79 Letter to Lucie Rommel, 27 December 1943, NA RG 242 T 84/275.

80 Paul Heider, 'Reaktionen in der Wehrmacht auf Gründung and Tätigkeit des Nationalkomitees "Freies Deutschland" und des Bundes Deutscher Offiziere' in Rolf Dieter Muller (ed), *Die Wehrmacht. Mythos und Realität* (Munich: 1999) p 623.

81 Hellmut Lang, `Tagesbericht´ (Rommel-Diktat), 20 March 1944, in *SDLC*, Roll 11.

82 Fröhlich, *Goebbels*, Vol II.12, 18 April 1944, p 129.

83 Hellmut Lang, `Tagesbericht´ (Rommel-Diktat), 13 May 1944, in *SDLC*, Roll 11.

84 Letter to Lucie Rommel, 12 May 1944, NA RG 242 T 84/275.

85 Letter to Lucie Rommel, 19 May 1944, NA RG 242 T 84/275.

86 'Befragung Jodls von 5. Juni 1946', *IMT*, p 441.

87 Below, *Adjutant*, p 375.

88 'Letter to Lucie Rommel, 18 June 1944' in Basil Henry Liddell Hart (ed), *The Rommel Papers* (London: 1953) p 492.

89 Ruge, 25 June 1944, in *SDLC*, Roll 2.

90 Ruge, 25 June 1944, in *SDLC*, Roll 2.

91 Ruge, 1 July 1944, in *SDLC*, Roll 2.

92 'Betrachtungen zur Lage', 15 July 1944, in Dieter Ose, *Entscheidung im Westen 1944. Der Oberbefehlshaber West und die Abwehr der alliierten Invasion* (Stuttgart: 1982) Appendix 15, p 335.

93 'Bericht über die Verwundung des OB der Heeresgruppe B', BA-MA, RH 19 IX/1.

94 Lang, `Tagesbericht´ (Rommel-Diktat), 21 July 1944, in *SDLC*, Roll 11.

95 Letter to Lucie Rommel, 24 July 1944, in *SDLC*, Roll 1.

96 Basil Henry Liddell Hart, *Jetzt dürfen sie reden. Hitlers Generale berichten* (Zürich: 1948) p 529.

97 Ruge, 21 July 1944, in *SDLC*, Roll 2.

Chapter 2

1 Hesse, 'Wandlung', in *SDLC*, Roll 3.

2 Letter to Lucie Rommel, 9 September 1939, NA RG 242 T 84/273.

3 OKW General Stabs Operationsabteilung, 10.2.1941, BA-MA, RH 2 v 459.

4 Letter to Lucie Rommel, 25 April 1941 in Liddell Hart, *Papers*, p 111.

5 Franz Halder, *Kriegstagebuch. Tagliche Aufzeichnungen des Chefs des Generalstabes des Heeres 1939-1942*, ed Arbeitskreis für Wehrforschung, Vol I–III (Stuttgart: 1962–64) Vol II, 23 April 1941, p 62f.

6 'Letter to Lucie Rommel, 25 April 1941' in Liddell Hart (ed), *Papers*, p 131.

7 Irving, *Rommel*, p 141.

8 Erwin Rommel, *Krieg ohne Hass*, ed Lucie-Marie Rommel and General Lieutenant Fritz Bayerlein (Heidenheim: 1953) p 390f.

9 Picker, *Tischgespräche*, 27 June 1942, p 388.

10 Leonidas E Hill (ed), *Die Weizsäcker-Papiere 1933-1950* (Frankfurt aM/Berlin/Wien: 1974) 29 June 1942, p 295.

11 Dwight D Eisenhower, *Kreuzzug in Europa* (Amsterdam: 1948) p 267.

12 Hitler, *Kampf*, p 73.

13 Rommel, *Krieg ohne Hass*, p 397.

14 Young, *Rommel*, p 141f.

15 Walter Baum and Eberhard Weichold, *Der Krieg der "Achsen-mächte" im Mittelmeer-Raum. Die "Strategie" der Diktatoren* (Zürich/Frankfurt: 1973) p 133f.

16 Schramm, *Kriegstagebuch,* Vol II, 4 July 1942, p 474.

17 Rommel, *Krieg ohne Hass*, p 383.

18 Letter from Rommel to Hitler, 16 March 1944, in *SDLC*, Roll 1.

19 Rommel, *Krieg ohne Hass*, p 385.

20 Lang, 'Tagesbericht' (Rommel-Diktat), 23 April 1944, in *SDLC*, Roll 11.

21 Hesse, 'Wandlung', in *SDLC*, Roll 3.

22 Reuth, *Rommel*, p 66.

23 Hesse, 'Wandlung', in *SDLC*, Roll 3.

24 Rommel, *Krieg ohne Hass*, p 394.

25 Harald Kuhn, *Viel Steine gab's und wenig Brot! Die Ereignisse im Frühjahr und Sommer 1941 in Libyens Wüste* (no date) p 68, hereafter Kuhn, *Libyens Wüste*.

26 Irving, *Rommel*, p 35f.

27 Below, *Adjutant*, p 13.

28 Kuhn, *Libyens Wüste*, p 69.

29 Johannes Streich, 'Erinnerungen an Afrika', in *SDLC*, Roll 3.

30 Letter from Brauchitsch to Rommel, 9 July 1941, in *SDLC*, Roll 1.

31 Fröhlich, *Goebbels*, Vol II.8, 11 May 1943, p 274.

32 Rommel, *Infanterie*, p 341f.

33 Galeazzo Ciano, *Tagebücher 1939-1943* (Bern: 1947) 27 December 1941, p 387.

34 Ciano, *Tagebücher*, 7 February 1942, p 402.

35 Ciano, *Tagebücher*, 22 June 1942, p 450.

36 Ralf Georg Reuth, *Entscheidung im Mittelmeer. Die südliche Peripherie Europas in der deutschen Strategie des Zweiten Weltkrieges 1940-1942* (Koblenz: 1985) p 121, note 24.

37 Ciano, *Tagebücher*, 27 September 1942, p 472.

38 Fröhlich, *Goebbels*, Vol II.8, 11 May 1943, p 274.

39 Fröhlich, *Goebbels*, Vol II.3, 31 March 1942, p 602.

Chapter 3

1 Picker, *Tischgespräche*, 22 June 1942, p 374.

2 Hitler, *Kampf*, p 187.

3 Curt Weithas, 'Das Sedan von St Valéry, June 1940 (Rundfunkbeitrag)', BA-MA, N 117/13.

4 *Der Gebirgler,* May/June 1940, BA-MA, N 117/13.

5 'Auf der Rommelbahn nachts um halb drei', BA-MA, N 117/17.

6 Weithas, 'St Valéry', BA-MA, N 117/13.

7 Hanns Gert von Esebeck, *Afrikanische Schicksalsjahre. Geschichte des Deutschen Afrikakorps unter Rommel* (Wiesbaden: 1950) p 16.

8 *Der Gebirgler,* May/June 1940, BA-MA, N 117/13.

9 *Der Gebirgler,* May/June 1940, BA-MA, N 117/13.

10 'Liebe Soldaten . . .', Heidenheim, December 1940 sowie die Anfrage ohne Datum, both BA-MA, N 117/13.

11 Esebeck, *Schicksalsjahre,* p 13f.

12 Zeitungsfragment vom 14 November 1942, BA-MA, N 117/15.

13 'Letter to Lucie Rommel, 8 April 1941' in Liddell Hart (ed), *Papers,* p 116.

14 Kuhn, *Libyens Wüste,* p 33.

15 Kuhn, *Libyens Wüste,* p 55.

16 Reuth, *Rommel,* p 85.

17 Reuth, *Rommel,* p 87.

18 Fröhlich, *Goebbels,* Vol II.2, 28 November 1941, p 385 (Reuth, *Goebbels,* Vol 4, p 1713f).

19 *Schwäbische Zeitung,* 5 April 1941, BA-MA, N 117/14.

20 *Adler im Süden* (date illegible), BA-MA, N 117/14.

21 *Westfälische Tageszeitung,* 16 January 1942, BA-MA, N 117/15.

22 United Press-Meldung, 23 January 1942, BA-MA, N 117/15.

23 Winston S Churchill, *Der Zweite Weltkrieg* (Bern/Munich: 1953) Vol 4.I, p 43f.

24 Churchill, *Weltkrieg,* Vol 4.I, p 87.

25 Esebeck, *Schicksalsjahre,* p 123n.

26 Esebeck, *Schicksalsjahre,* p 132.

27 Wolf Heckmann, *Rommels Krieg in Afrika. "Wüstenfüchse" gegen "Wüstenratten"* (Bergisch-Gladbach: 1976) p 301.

28 Fröhlich, *Goebbels,* Vol II.3, 7 February 1942, p 265.

29 Fröhlich, *Goebbels,* Vol II.3, 30 March 1942, p 580f.

30 Willi A Boelcke, *Wollt Ihr den totalen Krieg? Die geheimen Goebbels-Konferenzen 1939-1943* (Stuttgart: 1967), 29 January 1942, p 210f.

31 Boelcke, *Goebbels,* 5 February 1942, p 214.

32 *Marine Frontzeitung,* '. . .gegen Engeland', 25 January 1942, BA-MA, N 117/15.

33 *Völkischer Beobachter,* 22 June 1942, BA-MA, N 117/15.

34 *Chemnitzer Zeitung,* 23 June 1942, BA-MA, N 117/15.

35 Picker, *Tischgespräche*, 22 June 1942, p 373.
36 Picker, *Tischgespräche*, 9 July 1942, p 434.
37 Boelcke, *Goebbels*, 25 June 1942, p 252.
38 Albert Kesselring, *Soldat bis zum letzten Tag* (Bonn: 1953) p 169.
39 Reuth, *Entscheidung*, Appendix, Dok 13, p 250f.
40 *Völkischer Beobachter*, 3 October 1942, BA-MA, N 117/15.
41 Fröhlich, *Goebbels*, Vol II.6, 16 December 1942, p 453.
42 Churchill, *Weltkrieg*, Vol 4.II, p 70.
43 Churchill, *Weltkrieg*, Vol 4.II, p 64.
44 Alun Chalfont, *Montgomery. Rommels Gegenspieler* (Wiesbaden/Munich: 1976), p 180.
45 Boelcke, *Goebbels*, 6 November 1942, p 299.
46 Zeitungsausschnitt (ohne Titel), 14 November 1942, BA-MA, N 117/15.
47 Fröhlich, *Goebbels*, Vol II.8, 10 May 1943, p 266 (Reuth, *Goebbels*, Vol V, p 1931f).
48 Janusz Piekalkiewicz, *Der Wüstenkrieg in Africa 1940-1943* (Munich: n/a), p 268.
49 Alfred-Ingemar Berndt, '27 Monate Kampf in Afrika. Ein Rundfunkbeitrag', BA-MA, N 117/20.
50 Alfred-Ingemar Berndt, '27 Monate Kampf in Afrika. Ein Rundfunkbeitrag', p 29, BA-MA, N 117/20.
51 Fröhlich, *Goebbels*, Vol II.10, 27 October 1943, p 180.
52 Irving, *Rommel*, p 473.
53 *Die Zeit,* 10 May 1944.
54 Irving, *Rommel*, p 505.
55 Irving, *Rommel*, p 505.
56 Fröhlich, *Goebbels*, Vol II.4, 5 May 1942, p 241.

Chapter 4

1 Manfred Overesch (ed), *Das Dritte Reich 1933-1939. Eine Tagechronik der Politik, Wirtschaft und Kultur* (Düsseldorf: 1982) 2 February 1934, p 152.
2 Irving, *Rommel*, p 599.
3 Wilhelm von Schramm, *Aufstand der Generale. Der 20. Juli in Paris* (Munich: 1964) p 48.
4 Irving, *Rommel*, p 466.
5 Ruge, 25 June 1944, in *SDLC*, Roll 2.
6 Ulrich Heinemann, 'Caesar von Hofacker – Stauffenbergs Mann in

Paris' in Klemens Klemperer, Enrico Syring, Rainer Zitelmann (eds), *Für Deutschland. Die Männer des 20. Juli* (Frankfurt aM/Berlin: 1994) p 115.

7 Manfred Schmid, 'Caesar von Hofacker. Der 20. Juli in Paris' in Michael Bosch, Wolfgang Niess (eds), *Der Widerstand im deutschen Südwesten 1933-45* (Stuttgart: 1984), p 213.

8 'Kaltenbrunner-Bericht vom 4.8.1944' in Hans Adolf Jacobsen (ed), *Spiegelbild einer Verschwörung. Die Opposition gegen Hitler und der Staatsstreich vom 20. Juli 1944 in der SD-Berichterstattung. Geheime Dokumente aus dem ehemaligen Reichssicherheitshauptsamt* (Stuttgart: 1984) Vol I, p 136.

9 'Kaltenbrunner-Bericht vom 12.12.1944' in Jacobsen, *Verschwörung*, Vol I, p 521.

10 'Kaltenbrunner-Bericht vom 15.12.1944' in Jacobsen, *Verschwörung*, Vol I, p 529.

11 Maurice Philip Remy, *Mythos Rommel* (Munich: 2002) p 277.

12 *IMT*, Vol XII, 25 April 1946, p 269.

13 'Kaltenbrunner-Bericht vom 4.8.1944' in Jacobsen, *Verschwörung*, Vol I, p 136.

14 Max Domarus (ed), *Hitler. Reden und Proklamationen 1932-45* (Wiesbaden: 1973) Vol II.2, 20 July 1944, p 2118.

15 Ernst Jünger, *Strahlungen* (Tübingen: 1949) 31 May 1944, p 526.

16 Fröhlich, *Goebbels*, Vol II.13, 3 August 1944, p 208.

17 Fröhlich, *Goebbels*, Vol II.13, 3 August 1944, p 210.

18 Jodl Tagebuch, 1 August 1944, BA-MA, N 6922.

19 Warlimont, *Hauptquartier*, Fragment Nr 46, 31 August 1944, p 482.

20 Reuth, *Rommel*, p 154.

21 Halder, *Kriegstagebuch*, Vol III, 6 July 1941, p 48.

22 Brief Rahns vom 6 March 1972, BA-MA, N 117/34.

23 Reuth, *Rommel*, p 116f.

24 Gustave M Gilbert, *Nürnberger Tagebuch* (Frankfurt aM: 1962) p 96.

25 Ruge, 13 July 1944, in *SDLC*, Roll 2.

26 Ruge, 13 July 1944, in *SDLC*, Roll 2.

27 Ruge, 13 July 1944, in *SDLC*, Roll 2.

28 Ruge, 4 July 1944, in *SDLC*, Roll 2.

29 *IMT*, Vol X, 25 March 1946, p 68.

30 Letter from Schmundt to Rommel, 26 June 1944, in *SDLC*, Roll 1.

31 Letter from Rommel to Hitler, 1 October 1944, BA-MA, N 117/32.

32 Letter from Kronmüller to Bormann, 19 September 1944, Abschrift, N 117/29.

33 Martin Bormann, 'Aktenvermerk', 28 September 1944, BA-MA, N 117/29

34 Martin Bormann, 'Aktenvermerk', 28 September 1944, BA-MA, N 117/29

35 Heinrich Kirchheim, 'Eidesstattliche Erklärung, 16 September 1946' in *SDLC*, Roll 4.

36 Heinrich Kirchheim, 'Eidesstattliche Erklärung, 16 September 1946' in *SDLC*, Roll 4.

37 Hans Speidel, 'Aufzeichnung vom 10 August 1965' in *SDLC*, Roll 4.

38 Irving, *Rommel*, p 580.

39 Irving, *Rommel*, p 590.

40 Below, *Adjutant*, p 389.

41 Hermann Aldinger, 'Aussage vom 27./28.6. und 4.7.1949' in Ernst Maisel, *Spruchkammerverfahren*, Staatsarchiv München (herafter STAM), Ka 1112.

42 Rommel, *Krieg ohne Hass*, p 401.

43 Ruge, 4 July 1944, in *SDLC*, Roll 2.

44 'Letter from Kluge to Hitler, 18 August 1944' in Ose, *Entscheidung*, Anlage 18, p 339f.

45 *Südkurier*, 16 October 1945.

46 Hermann Aldinger, 'Aussage' in Maisel, *Spruchkammerverfahren*, STAM, Ka 1112.

47 *Südkurier*, 8 September 1945. The so-called 'Riedlinger Erklärung' by Manfred Rommel is dated 27 April 1945.

48 Heinrich Doose, 'Aussage' 30 May 1945, BA-MA, N 117/29.

49 Kurt Wendt, *Finale der Invasion. Warum? 2. Teil* (Hamburg: 1985) p 170.

50 Reuth, *Rommel*, p 128.

51 Below, *Adjutant*, p 390.

52 Befragung Manfred Rommels durch David Irving, 7 June 1975, in *SDLC*, Roll 3.

53 'Generalfeldmarschall Rommel zum Gedenken. 15. November 1981 – 14. Oktober 1944' , ohne Datum und Ort, S. 21, in *SDLC*, Roll 3.

54 'Generalfeldmarschall Rommel zum Gedenken. 15. November 1981 – 14. Oktober 1944', ohne Datum und Ort, S. 42, in *SDLC*, Roll 3.

55 Young, *Rommel*, p 257.

Chapter 5

1 *Südkurier,* 8 September 1945.
2 *Südkurier,* 16 October 1945.
3 *Südkurier,* 16 October 1945.
4 'Erklärung von Lucie Rommel vom 9 September 1945', BA-MA, N 558/77.
5 Eugen Kogon, 'Das deutsche Volk und die Konzentrationslager – seit 1945' in Eugen Kogon, *Der SS-Staat* (Frankfurt aM: 1961) p 403.
6 Hans Speidel, *Invasion 1944. Der Letzte Chef des Generalstabes von Feldmarschall Rommel über die Invasion und das Schicksal seines Oberbefehlshabers* (Frankfurt aM/Berlin/Vienna: 1979) p 144.
7 Leo Freiherr Geyr von Schweppenburg, 'Eidesstattliche Erklärung vom 27 April 1960' in *SDLC*, Roll 3.
8 *Christ und Welt,* 25 September 1948.
9 Speidel, *Invasion*, p 133. The first edition of Speidel's book (Tübingen/ Stuttgart: 1949) had the subtitle: *Ein Beitrag zu Rommels und des Reiches Schicksal.*
10 Jünger, *Strahlungen*, Vorwort p 13.
11 Young, *Rommel*, p 259.
12 *Amt Blank* was the predecessor of the German Ministry of Defence during a time when the rearmament of the Federal Republic of Germany had already been decided by the former enemies and future allies, but the treaties to that effect had not yet been ratified.
13 Remy, *Mythos*, p 8.
14 'Manfred Rommel an David Irving, 13 November 1974' in *SDLC*, Roll 4.
15 Dieter Ose, 'Erwin Rommel' in Rudolf Lill, Heinrich Oberreuther (eds) *20. Juli – Porträts des Widerstands* (Munich: 1989) pp 253–268.
16 David Fraser, *Rommel. Die Biographie* (Berlin: 1995) p 503f.
17 Ralph Giordano, *Die Traditionslüge. Vom Kriegerkult in der Bundeswehr* (Cologne: 2000), p 317.
18 Rudolf Gültner, 'Das Idol' in Guido Knopp, *Hitlers Krieger* (Munich: 1998) pp 15–92.

Bibliography

English editions of German works follow the German title in
square brackets

By Erwin Rommel

Rommel, Erwin, *Infanterie greift an. Erlebnis und Erfahrung* (Potsdam:
1941) [*Infantry Attacks*, tr Lt Col G E Kiddé (Infantry Journal,
Washington DC: 1944)].
——————————, *Krieg ohne Hass*, Lucie Maria Rommel, General
Lieutenant Fritz Bayerlein (eds) (Heidenheim: 1955).
——————————, *The Rommel Papers*, eds Liddell Hart, Basil Henry,
Lucie Maria Rommel, Manfred Rommel, Fritz Bayerlein, tr
Paul Findlay (Collins, London: 1953).

By others

Aberger, Heinz-Dietrich, *Die 5. (lei)/21. Panzer-Division in Nord-afrika
1941-1943* (Reutlingen: 1994).
Ansel, Walter, *Hitler and the Middle Sea* (Duke University Press,
Durham NC: 1972).
Bargatzki, Walter, *Hotel Majestic. Ein Deutscher im besetzten Frankreich*
(Freiburg i. Brsg: 1987)
Barnett, Corelli, *Wüsten-Generale* (Hannover: 1961) [*The Desert
Generals* (William Kimber & Co, London: 1960)].
Bayerlein, Fritz, 'Rommel. Eine Würdigung seiner Persönlichkeit' in
Verband ehemaliger Angehöriger Deutsches Afrikakorps e. V.
with Rommel-Sozialwerk (eds), *Schicksal Nordafrika* (Döffingen:
1954).
Behrendt, Hans-Otto, *Rommels Kenntnis vom Feind im Afrika-feldzug .
Ein Bericht über die Feindnachrichtenarbeit, insbesondere die*

235

Funkaufklärung (Freiburg: 1980) [*Rommel's Intelligence in the Desert Campaign* (Kimber, London: 1985)].

Below, Nikolaus von, *Als Hitlers Adjutant 1937-1945* (Mainz: 1980).

Boelcke, Willi A, *Wollt Ihr den totalen Krieg? Die geheimen Goebbels-Konferenzen 1939-1943* (Stuttgart: 1967) [*The Secret Conferences of Dr. Goebbels, October 1939 –March 1943*, tr Ewald Osers (Weidenfield & Nicholson, London: 1970)].

Broszat, Martin, 'Soziale Motivation und Führer-Bindung des Nationalsozialismus' in *Vierteljahreshefte für Zeitgeschichte* 18 (1970) p 393 ff.

Bücheler, Heinrich, *Karl-Heinrich von Stülpnagel. Soldat, Philosoph, Verschwörer* (Berlin: 1989).

Burdick, Charles B, *Unternehmen Sonnenblume. Der Entschluss zum Afrika-Feldzug* (Neckargmünd: 1972).

Carell, Paul, *Die Wüstenfüchse. Mit Rommel in Afrika* (Hamburg: 1958) [*Foxes of the Desert*, tr Mervyn Savill (MacDonald, London: 1960)].

_____, *Sie kommen!* (Gütersloh: 1960) [*Invasion: They're Coming!*, tr E Osers (Harrap: London: 1962)].

Chalfont, Alun, *Montgomery of Alamein* (Weidenfeld & Nicholson, London: 1976).

Ciano, Galeazzo, *Tagebücher 1939–1943* (Bern: 1947) [*Diary, 1939-1943* (Enigma Books, New York: 2002)].

Cordier, Sherwood S, 'Erwin Rommel. A Study in Command' in *Armor* 69 (Washington, DC: 1960), Nr 5, p 15 ff.

Eisenhower, Dwight D, *Kreuzzug in Europa* (Amsterdam: 1948) [*Crusade in Europe* (Doubleday, New York: 1948)].

Esebeck, Hanns Gert Freiherr von, *Afrikanische Schicksalsjahre. Geschichte des Deutschen Afrikakorps unter Rommel* (Wiesbaden: 1961).

Fest, Joachim C, *Plotting Hitler's Death: The Story of the German Resistance*, tr Bruce Little (New York: 1996).

Forty, George, *Africa-Korps at War* (Vol I), *The Road to Alexandria* (Vol II) (Scribner, New York: 1978).

Fourie, Deon, 'Rommel – One of the Great Captains of History' in *Kommando* 14 (1963) Nr 9, p 18 ff.

Fraser, David, *Rommel. Die Biographie* (Berlin: 1995) [*Knight's Cross: A Life of Field Marshal Erwin Rommel* (HarperCollins, New York: 1993)].

Gause, Alfred, 'Der Feldzug in Nordafrika im Jahre 1942' in *Wehrwissenschaftliche Rundschau,* 12/1962, p 654 ff.

Geyr von Schweppenburg, Leo Freiherr, 'Some More Facts About Rommel' in *Kommando,* 15 (1964), Nr 1, p 17 ff.

Gilbert, Gustave M, *Nürnberger Tagebuch* (Frankfurt a.M.: 1962)
  [*Nuremberg Diary* (Farrar, Straus & Co, New York: 1947)].
Giordano, Ralph, *Die Traditionslüge. Vom Kriegerkult in der Bundeswehr*
  (Köln: 2000).
Guderian, Heinz, *Panzer Leader*, tr Constantine Fitzgibbon (Dutton,
  New York: 1952).
Gültner, Rudolf, 'Das Idol' in Guido Knopp, *Hitlers Krieger*
  (München: 1998) pp 15–92.
Gundelach, Karl, *Die deutsche Luftwaffe im Mittelmeer 1940-1945*
  (Frankfurt aM: 1981).
Halder, Franz, *Kriegstagebuch 1939-1942* Bd. I–III (Stuttgart 1962–4)
  [*The Private War Journals of Colonel General Franz Halder*
  (Westview Press, Boulder, Colorado: 1976)].
Heckmann, Wolf, *Rommels Krieg in Afrika* (Bergisch-Gladbach: 1976)
  [*Rommel's War in Africa*, tr Stephen Seago (Doubleday, New
  York: 1981)].
Heider, Paul, 'Reaktionen in der Wehrmacht auf Gründung und
  Tätigkeit des Nationalkomitees "Freies Detuschland" und des
  Bundes Deutscher Offiziere' in Rolf-Dieter Müller, Hans-Erich
  Volkmann (eds), *Die Wehrmacht. Mythos und Realität* (München:
  1999) .
Hesse, Kurt, 'Rommel und der Geist von Potsdam' in *Die Oase* 18
  (Bochum: 1968) Nr 3, p 3 f.
Heusinger, Adolf, *Befehl im Widerstreit. Schicksalsstunden der deutschen
  Armee 1923-1945* (Tübingen/ Stuttgart: 1950).
Hillgruber, Andreas, 'England in Hitlers aussenpolitischer
  Konzeption' in Andreas Hillgruber, *Deutsche Grossmacht- und
  Weltpolitik im 19. und 20. Jahrhundert* (Düsseldorf: 1977) p 180
  ff.
Irving, David, *Rommel. Eine Biographie* (Hamburg: 1978) [*The Trail of
  the Fox* (Dutton, New York: 1977)].
Jacobsen, Hans-Adolf (ed), *Spiegelbild einer Verschwörung. Die Opposition
  gegen Hitler und der Staatsstreich vom 20. Juli 1944 in der SD-
  Berichterstattung. Geheime Dokumente aus dem ehemaligen
  Reichssicherheitshauptamt* (Stuttgart: 1984) Vols I and II.
Jäckel, Eberhard, *Hitlers Weltanschauung. Entwerf einer Herrschaft*
  (Tübingen: 1949) [*A Blueprint for Power*, tr Herbert Arnold
  (Wesleyan University Press, Middletown, Connecticut: 1972)].
Jünger, Ernst, *Strahlungen* (Tübingen: 1949).
Kesselring, Albert, *Soldat bis zum letzen Tag* (Bonn: 1953) [*Kesselring: A
  Soldier's Diary*, tr Lynton Hudson (William Morrow, NY: 1954)].
Klemens, Klemperer, Enrico Syring, Rainer Zitelmann (eds), *Für
  Deutschland. Die Männer des 20. Juli* (Frankfurt aM: 1994)

237

Knopp, Guido, *Hitlers Krieger* (München: 1998).

Koch, Lutz, *Erwin Rommel. Die Wandlung eines grossen Soldaten* (Stuttgart: 1950).

Kogon, Eugen, 'Das deutsche Volk und die Konzentrationslager – seit 1945' in Eugen Kogon, *Der SS-Staat* (Frankfurt aM: 1961).

Kuhn, Harald, *Viel Steine gab's und wenig Brot! Die Ereignisse im Frühjahr und Sommer 1941 in Libyens Wüste* (n/a: n/a).

Kurowski, Franz, *Endkampf in Nordafrika. Der Opfergang der Heeresgruppe Rommel in Tunesien 1942/3* (Leoni: 1983).

Lewin, Ronald, *Rommel* (Stuttgart: 1969) [*Rommel as Military Commander* (Batsford, London: 1968)].

Liddell Hart, Basil Henry, *Jetzt dürfen sie reden. Hitlers Generale berichten* (Zürich: 1948) [*The Other Side of the Hill* (Cassell, London: 1948)].

Maurès, Didier, *Erwin Rommel* (Paris: 1968).

Meyer, Hans R, *Sand in den Augen. Die Afrika Soldaten* (Heusenstamm: 1997).

Montgomery, Bernard Law, 'A Worthy Foe' in *Life Atlantic* 45, September 2 (Paris: 1968) Nr 5, p 48 ff.

Ose, Dieter, *Entscheidung im Westen 1944. Der Oberbefehlshaber West und die Abwehr der alliierten Invasion* (Stuttgart: 1982).

_____, 'Erwin Rommel' in Rudolf Lill, Heinrich Oberreuther (eds) *20. Juli – Porträts des Widerstands* (München: 1989).

Piekalkiewicz, Janusz, *Der Wüstenkrieg in Afrika 1940-43* (München: 1985).

Remy, Maurice Philip, *Mythos Rommel* (München: 2002).

Reuth, Ralf Georg, *Entscheidung im Mittelmeer. Die südliche Peripherie Europas in der deutschen Strategie des Zweiten Weltkrieges 1940-42* (Koblenz: 1985).

_____, *Goebbels. Eine Biographie* (München: 1990). [*Goebbels*, tr Krishna Winston (Harcourt Brace, New York: 1993)].

_____, *Hitler. Eine politische Biographie* (München: 2003).

_____, *Rommel. Des Führers General* (München: 1987).

Rommel, Manfred, 'Rommel und der Führerbefehl' in *Die Oase* 8 (Bochum: 1958) Nr 5, p 6.

Ruge, Friedrich, *Rommel und die Invasion. Erinnerungen* (Stuttgart: 1959) [*Rommel in Normandy: Reminiscences*, tr Ursula R Moessner (Presidio Press, San Rafael CA: 1979)].

Saurel, Louis, *Rommel* (Paris: 1967).

Schmidt, Heinz Werner, *Mit Rommel in Afrika* (München: 1951) [*With Rommel in the Desert* (Harrap, London: 1951)].

Schramm, Percy Ernst (ed), *Kriegstagebuch des Oberkommandos der Wehrmacht (Wehrmachtführungsstab)* (München: 1982), Vols I – IV.

Schramm, Wilhelm von, *Aufstand der Generale. Der 20. Juli in Paris* (München: 1964).

Schreiber, Gerhard, 'Der Mittelmeerraum in Hitlers Strategie 1940. "Programm" und militärische Planung' in *Militärgeschichtliche Mitteilungen* 2 (1980) p 69 ff.

Schweyher, Karl, *1941-1942 Libyen – Ägypten – Tunesien* (Nerphen: 1994).

Speidel, Hans, *Aus unserer Zeit. Erinnerungen* (Wien: 1977).

_____, *Invasion 1944. Ein Beitrag zu Rommels und des Reiches Schicksal* (Stuttgart: 1949) [*Invasion 1944: Rommel and the Normandy Campaign*, tr Theo R Crevenne (Henry Regnery, Chicago: 1950)].

_____, *Invasion 1944. Der letzte Chef des Generalstabes von Feldmarschall Rommel über die Invasion und das Schicksal seines Oberbefehlshabers* (Frankfurt aM/ Berlin/ Wien: 1979).

Taysen, Adalbert von, *Tobruk 1941. Der Kampf um in Nord-afrika* (Freiburg: 1976).

Theil, Edmund, *Rommels verheizte Armee. Der Kampf der Heeresgruppe Afrika von El Alamein bis Tunis* (München: 1979).

Warlimont, Walter, 'Die Entscheidung im Mittelmeer 1942' in Hans Adolf Jacobsen, Jürgen Rohwer (eds), *Entscheidungsschlachten des Zweiten Weltkrieges* (Frankfurt aM: 1960) p 233 ff.

_____, *Im Hauptquartier der deutschen Wehrmacht 1939–1945* (Bonn: 1964) [*Inside Hitler's Headquarters 1939–1945*, tr R H Barry (F A Praeger, New York: 1964)].

Weichold, Eberhard, 'Die deutsche Führung und das Mittelmeer unter dem Blickwinkel der Seestrategie' in *Wehrwissenschaftliche Rundschau* 9 (1959) Issue 3, p 164 ff.

Wendt, Kurt, *Finale der Invasion, Warum?, 2. Teil* (Hamburg: 1985).

Westphal, Siegfried, *Erinnerungen* (Frankfurt aM: 1975).

_____, *The German Army in the West* (Cassell, London: 1951).

Westphal, Siegfried, *Macht als vorwärts, Jungs!* (Bad Wiessee: 1960).

Zur Mühlen, Bengt von, *Die Angeklagten des 20. Juli vor dem Volksgerichtshof* (Berlin: 2001).

Index

244